I can start your business

Everything you need to know to run your limited company or self employment – for locums, contractors, freelancers and small business

Updated for 2019/20 tax year

Russell Smith

Managing Director, RS Accountancy

www.rsaccountancy.co.uk

Free tax, accounts and profit review with customised action plan worth £200 for readers at www.rsaccountancy.co.uk

Contents

Author's note

When I turned 26 years old, my current employer didn't let me go on holiday to see my brother get married in Australia.

Fed up with someone else dictating the course of my life (well, holiday schedule), I resigned as a finance accountant from a large multi-national company and set up my own business.

I decided that the best chance of running a successful business would be to start an accountancy practice (based on the fact that I was a chartered accountant). Sadly, in my 19 years of becoming an accountant (from beginning maths at the age of 5), I had forgotten to learn anything about sales and marketing.

Bad mistake.

After two months, my accountancy skills were red hot but my client number was zero - Ouch.

No clients, no income, no business.

That was 10 years ago and since then I have worked with 400 clients and managed a team of 10 people.

Why am I telling you this?

Because I'm not a professional author. I'm a chartered accountant who knows how to start and grow a business.

That means that there will be times when those eagle-eyed readers might notice a grammar or spelling error.

If you want a book written by an accountant who has no experience in running a business then I can give you a bucket-load of recommendations. If you want someone who has been exactly where you are – at the beginning, then read on…..

By the way, any purchaser of this book is entitled to a free tax, accounts and profit review worth £200. Send me an email on russell@rsaccountancy.co.uk

Introduction

Your business finances: Why do you need to know and what do you need to know?

I hate IT.

I pretty much hate anything to do with computers. I always have but unfortunately when you are running a business you have to use computers and know something about them.

I did know this when I started my first business, an accountancy practice, but I seemed to ignore the fact that I really should know something about them. OK, I wasn't completely in the dark. I did know how to use them for my work (especially spreadsheets) but anything to do with networking, servers, backups – totally clueless!

So after being in denial for quite a while, I knew I had to do something. So I did. I hired an IT firm to 'sort out' my IT. They were a good local firm, pretty big and seemed like they would give me a great service. However, after the initial meeting I realised one thing. They would help me with my IT in my growing business but they were not the magic wand I was looking for. Essentially, I wanted to hand everything to them and for them to just take the problem away.

Despite me giving them a monthly fee, this was not going to happen for two reasons. Firstly, they wanted to meet me every quarter and speak to me on the phone about IT and secondly, I didn't understand what they were saying. They wanted me to be involved in the process but I did not want anything to do with it.

What was worse was that we now had multiple computers in the business which meant my team were asking me questions when things went wrong, which they did – often! It was the blind leading the blind since I had no clue where to start and whilst the IT firm were going to help me they would not be able to cope with my ignorance.

So I made a decision. I needed to understand something about IT. I didn't need to be an expert, I just needed a level of knowledge about IT to be able to communicate to my IT firm and to be able to understand how IT was helping me grow my business.

The next day, I bought one of those yellow 'IT for dummies' type books, sat down in my 'reading chair' and read the damn thing cover to cover in about four hours. Boring though it was (and believe me......it was!), I emerged from my chair with my IT knowledge increased tenfold. Ok, I wasn't an expert but I now understood what my IT guy was speaking about.

As much as I (still) absolutely hate IT, I love tax, accountancy and business finances. I have been doing this work for close to twenty years and can't get enough of it. My guess is that you do not feel the same about your business finances. For you, it may be a stress, a chore, an inconvenience, not in your flow, not your idea of fun, a pain in the neck, something someone else can do.

I'm here to tell you that:

EVEN THOUGH YOU MAY NOT LIKE THE IDEA OF BUSINESS FINANCES – YOU HAVE TO KNOW SOME OF THIS STUFF!

If you want to grow a business, create wealth for yourself and have a generally happy life, you have to understand about business finances.

Why? Simply put, finances (or maths) is the language of business. Understanding this, can save you lots of unnecessary pain.

Growing and running a profitable business involves 3 things. Marketing and selling a product or service, delivering the product or service in an efficient, timely way that pleases your customers and managing the finances to ensure you are making a profit and generating cash.

It is highly unlikely that you will be good at all 3 but you MUST understand all 3. You do not want to outsource 100% of this to someone who tells you they know what they are doing (especially in the area of finances).

The good news is, as someone who loves being an accountant, I'm here to tell you that you don't need to become an accountant. The aim of this book is to tell you in simple, jargon-free terms what you need to know (and what you don't).

Getting a decent accountant and bookkeeper is one of the biggest decisions you can make in business and whilst it is true these nice people will help you in your finances, they will need you to play your part as well. You need a level of understanding. So I am here to give you what you need!

You'll quickly see that I'm not the next Ian McEwan, JK Rowling or Thomas Hardy. I'm not writing this book to win literary awards, I'm writing this to explain in as simple terms as I can, what you need to know about your business finances. So you may find that some of the language is at times – colloquial. However, I hope you find this an easy read on a subject that most people find difficult to grasp.

I have used the abbreviation HMRC throughout the book for 'Her Majesty's Revenue & Customs'. HMRC is the government department that deals with all the taxes. The government sets the tax rates, HMRC's job is to collect it. My job as an accountant is to make sure you comply with the tax law without needlessly overpaying tax.

If you have liked what you have read here, or there is something that you want further clarification on, feel free drop me an email on: russell@rsaccountancy.co.uk.

I also blog every day on www.rsaccountancy.co.uk/daily-blog and you can see me on Twitter @russellstweets and @rsaccountancy

Chapter 1 – Finance basics

This chapter is going to tell you everything that you should know about your business finances. You know when you are at a seminar and the presenter says, there are no dumb questions. Well, this is the chapter with the dumb questions. If you read this chapter, not only will you not look dumb at a seminar but you could potentially see your business in a completely different light.

What is profit?

I'm now going to tell you what profit is, which I'm sure you know. Then I'm going to tell you what profit REALLY is.

What profit is…

Profit is:

Turnover

Minus all expenses

= Profit

Turnover is your sales, specifically your sales invoices (not your income from sales – more on this later).

All expenses is everything you have been invoiced for in the business. All your costs that you have in running your business e.g. team, rent, marketing, accountancy (hooray), IT (ugh) etc.

Profit is what is left over.

Turnover and expenses should <u>not</u> have VAT included (unless you are on the flat rate scheme more on this later).

Here's what profit really is….

Profit is the life-blood of your existence as a business owner.

Profit is the single most important reason you are in business and the most important thing in the business.

Unfortunately, it is not particularly fashionable to say this at this time. It's probably because if you are British like me, there is a general distrust of people getting rich and it is not polite to talk about money and profit. But whilst I'm not asking you to shout about it, I am asking you realise and focus on the fact that PROFIT IS EVERYTHING!!!

OK, it is true to say that if you have to annoy your customers, kill the environment and make your employees sweat in the pursuit of profit, then this is not a good thing (obviously). Other than morally wrong, it is not sustainable.

But don't get mixed up on society's anti-profit rhetoric to cloud the fact that:

YOU ARE IN BUSINESS TO MAKE MONEY!

The purpose of a business is not to have fun, make friends or make the world a better place, the point of a business is make profit. If you can have fun and have an impact on the world for the better then that's great, but primarily your business is about profit.

If you are reading this, thinking 'hmmmmm, I'm not sure about this', then let me kill the argument in one sentence:

'No profit = no business'

This sentence even applies to non-profit organisations and charities. If you are not making the surpluses of income over expenses you will not be around for long.

(For the pedants out there, it is true that some businesses make losses for years before they 'turn' a profit. They only do this because they have massive cash funding behind them and it is not something I recommend to any small business unless you are the next Jeff Bezos. As far as I can see, if you are not making a profit, you are not in business. Period.)

Profit is 'what is left over'

Like me, I'm sure you've had times when you have had money at the beginning of the month and 30 days later you've wondered where all the money has gone. (I said 'like me' but the reality is I have reconciled my bank account for 20 years – I know exactly where my money is going but hey, I'm an accountant and I'm not claiming to have a life).

Profit is the same thing. It can disappear in a cloud of expenditure. If you spend too much in the business then your profit will disappear. So, you must keep an eye on your costs.

A quick tip on how to get around this, is to set a profit target and not ever let your income minus expenditure get lower than this number. Simple, but effective.

How to make more profit

This is a huge subject and one for a future book but let me give you three quick tips on this.

Tip no. 1 - Understand the different type of expenses

Firstly, there are two types of expenses. There are (jargon alert) 'cost of sales' and 'overheads'. Cost of sales or sometimes called 'direct costs' are those costs in the business that directly impact the sales. For example, if you are making pens, then ink would be a direct cost. If you run a restaurant, food will be a direct cost. Direct costs are directly attributable to sales which means if your sales go up, your direct costs should go up. If your sales go down, then your direct costs will go down.

Overheads are costs that happen whether or not you are making sales. A good example is rent. If you move into an office or warehouse but you don't actually do any work or production, you still have to pay your landlord. It's the same with your IT supplier, accountant and other fixed costs. They are fixed because they are going to happen with no relation to your sales. The trick with overheads is not to get them too high especially in the early days.

There is a cost that is in-between 'cost of sales' and 'direct costs' and that is your team i.e. wages and salaries. This can be an overhead since you have to pay your team whether or not you make any sales but at the same time, if you are a service company such as a marketing agency then your team would be a direct cost since they generate sales.

To add to the confusion, in your Companies House year-end accounts that your accountant will prepare, this cost would appear in 'overheads'.

To make it simple, if you are a service company (you are selling services rather than products) then I would put them in direct costs (except for the admin staff, put those in overheads). However, if you make a product, put all team costs in overheads.

Tip no. 2 - Understand break-even

Break-even is where your profit is zero. This means that you have made enough sales to cover all your expenses. It is the 'no man's land' between loss and profit. The aim of business is to break even and then tip it into profit.

Here is what the break-even looks like:

Turnover	£10,000
Expenses	£10,000
Profit	0

Again, the trick is to have a profit target, so in this case, if your profit target is £2,000, your turnover needs to be £2,000 more than your expenses.

Tip no. 3 - Decide what to focus on

When I sit down with clients to find out how they can make more profit, the meetings usually last one hour at a time. If I was to sit down with you for one hour, I would probably spend 35 minutes on your pricing, 20 minutes on your efficiency of delivery of your product or service and 5 minutes on your overheads.

It is good to know and review your overheads but you are not going to get rich by cutting everything. There is a limit to how low you can get your costs. Conversely, there is no limit to your pricing/turnover so most of your time should be concentrated on how to sell more rather than how to sell more efficiently.

Where does the business owner cost go in the profit calculation?

Later on in this book, I will tell you how to pay yourself in a tax efficient way which is essentially a minimal salary of £12,500 (which does appear as a business cost) and dividends £37,500 (which does not).

However, if we just ignore how it looks in your Companies House year-end accounts for now, we have two choices. We can put your cost as business owner into the costs or leave out.

There isn't really a right or wrong answer to this but I'm going to argue that you put your cost in for the following reasons:

1. It shows your TRUE profit since you are a cost to the business
2. It is more accurate when you are looking at cash i.e. currently if you take out £5,000 a month from your business it shows up on your cash but not your profit
3. If you are sick and can't work, someone has got to do what you do therefore you will have to pay someone a salary.

My only caveat on this is that if you are a one person business and have no plans of expansion then you may as well just leave the cost out because essentially your profit is your earnings.

However, if you are planning to grow your business and employ a team then you should bring the cost in to really see whether your business is making profits or not.

What is cash?

Running a business is all about timing and this is no better illustrated than in managing your cash.

Cash is all about timing – do you have enough cash in your bank account to pay the people you owe, be they suppliers, team members or the tax man.

In the business, you can have a current account, a deposit account, credit cards, bank loans and even a bank overdraft.

However, the moment that you have to pay someone you owe and you can't, that's the point you are technically insolvent i.e. out of business. Of course, if you ever find yourself in this situation there are many options to get yourself out of it but if you are starting a business from scratch you don't want to be in this predicament. You want to always have cash in your business.

Some business owners skilfully run their business through an overdraft and by tracking their cash daily they manage to grow their business successfully. Whilst this can be done, the time spend and emotional/psychological drain on a business owner's mind can make it a very unpleasant experience and there is always the risk that the clock will catch up with them. Here's how this works.....

The difference between profit and cash

The business owner wants to grow the business so starts investing in marketing. The suppliers that this business owner is using have 30 day terms i.e. they want to be paid within 30 days. The marketing is successful and the sales roll in to the business. Turnover is up and the business owner is pleased.

Despite the heavy spend on marketing, the business owner is smart and is tracking the profit. Fortunately, the business is clearly making a profit and everybody is happy.

However, the business owner has made two miscalculations. Firstly, they have focussed entirely on profit and ignored cash and secondly, because of this, they have given their customers 60 days terms i.e given the customer 60 days to pay the sales invoices. So right from the start of the business there will be a cash hole i.e. the business is paying their suppliers in 30 days and receiving the cash in 60 days.

This isn't the end of the world if the business owner had invested some cash in the business at the start, what accountants would call 'working capital'. But if they haven't, they are faced with the confusing situation of patting themselves on the back for all the profit they made and then realising they can't pay their suppliers.

Faced with angry calls from suppliers and then even scarier calls and letters from HM Revenue & Customers the business owner does two things to try and rectify the situation. Firstly, they review their credit control procedures and start tightening up on the systems to ensure the customers are paying them on time and secondly, they boost the marketing spend to increase the sales to trade more and therefore make more profit.

Both are misjudgements which will lead to a financial catastrophe. Firstly, whilst it is good for the credit control procedures to be improved, the customers are still paying on 60 days which is 30 days more than they are paying suppliers. Secondly, it is possible to trade out of a financial crisis but more than likely, the problem will become bigger. The problem isn't profit or selling, the problem is a timing difference on cash. Even if the business owner had money invested at the start, any increase in trade with this sort of mismatch will lead to more cash needed to keep the business afloat.

This problem is all too common and sadly we accountants don't always help much! Firstly, the year-end accounts that we produce for Companies House don't really tell you about profit. We could give you a 'cash flow statement' which shows you the link between profit and cash (it is all about timing) but they won't really tell you too much about how to correct the situation.

Secondly, because we as accountants are obsessed with profit, sometimes the whole cash situation is not even picked up on. I can tell you many stories of how year-end accounts have been technically correct from an accounting perspective but utterly useless in telling a business owner where they stand cash-wise.

So given this problem, here are 3 tips:

Tip no. 1 – Play the profit game and play the cash game

See the profit game and the cash game as two separate games. They are linked but you will need an accountancy degree to link the two so don't bother. The game is to hit your profit target AND your cash target.

I'll tell you now, it is a frustrating experience. It is like playing Minecraft whilst playing Angry Birds at the same time. You've got to keep both plates spinning at the same time and you must give equal time and attention to both.

Tip no. 2 – You can run an unprofitable business and have cash in the bank, but you can also run a profitable business and have no cash

Again, this is about timing.

If your customers pay you before you pay your suppliers then you are likely to have cash in the bank despite being unprofitable (mainly because HM Revenue & Customs give you very favourable terms on paying tax – more on this later).

However, if your business is fundamentally unprofitable, no amount of work on improving your cash flow will change this fact. It will catch up with you.

If your business is profitable and your cash collection procedures are suspect, you may still survive but it could be close.

Essentially, after writing a Chapter telling you that profit is everything, I'm now saying that whilst this is true, without cash you don't even get to play the game. You must have cash at all times and you cannot run out. No cash = no business.

You've probably heard this cliché many times (especially if you watch things like 'The Apprentice' where a budding entrepreneur will espouse this) but a cliché means 'overused truth' and I must admit this one really explains it well:

Turnover is *vanity*

Profit is *sanity*

Cash is *reality*

Tip no. 3 – If you start making profits and you are generating cash, don't take too much out

In later chapters, I will talk about how you can extract money from your business tax efficiently, for now I will just state that you don't want to be taking out more profit than you are making.

I have seen many businesses with struggling cash flow problems which actually are profitable. When I've looked a bit deeper, the business didn't actually have any problems with cash collection or even cash flow per se, the problem was the business owner was taking all the profit and more. Therefore, the business could never manage on its own two feet because all the cash was evaporating into the business owner's pocket!

What is a profit and loss account?

You can have two main sets of accounts. The year-end accounts that are prepared by an accountant for Companies House and the Tax office, and management accounts which are your own accounts that can be prepared quarterly, monthly or even weekly.

In the set of accounts for Companies House and the Tax office, there will always be a profit and loss account and balance sheet. For your own management accounts, it is wise to include a cash flow forecast.

The profit and loss account is perhaps the easiest to understand.

This is a very simple example of a profit and loss account:

Turnover	£100,000
Cost of sales	-£30,000
Gross profit	£70,000
Overheads	£40,000
Net profit	£30,000
Tax	£5,700

Profit after tax	£24,300

If you go back to my original chapter on profit, this is essentially showing you the turnover (sales) of the business, the two types of expenses: cost of sales (or sometimes called direct costs) and overheads, profit and crucially the tax on the profit (more on this later).

The only other jargon term I have included here is 'gross profit' which is essentially the profit after deducting cost of sales from turnover (but ignoring overheads). 'Net profit' is after all costs have been deducted – 'cost of sales' and 'overheads'. Profit after tax essentially means the profit that is available to the business owner.

The profit and loss account is NET of VAT i.e. VAT is NOT included.

Vat is a funny tax (strange not humorous). Essentially, you are collecting VAT from your customers, paying VAT to your suppliers and paying the balance over to HM Revenue & Customs. Based on the fact that businesses should be making profit i.e. charging more VAT than paying it out, the government gets the VAT bonus (£27 billion at the last count).

For a business owner, VAT is an annoying complication and I've written a whole chapter on it. For now, just make sure your sales and expenses ignore VAT.

The main benefit of the profit and loss account is quite simple, it tells you if you are making a profit or a loss. If you are making a profit it also tells you how much tax you have to pay.

What is a balance sheet?

Whilst most business owners do understand the profit and loss account, not many understand the balance sheet. I have to say, that (please don't let the accountancy gods strike me down for saying this) the balance sheet has limited use for business owners on a day to day basis. I would definitely rank it a distant third behind profit and loss account and the cash flow statement.

That said, if I am able to explain it in a non-accountancy way, then it would be good to understand (but not essential).

Accountancy, the recording of business transactions, is based on a practice called 'double-entry bookkeeping' which basically means every transaction is recorded twice so that nothing is missed.

The balance sheet is a check that everything has been recorded. So an accountant can tell that the profit and loss account is accurate if the balance sheet all ties up.

OK, that was in accountancy jargon, what really is a balance sheet?

The balance sheet tells you three things.

Firstly, it gives you a run-down of all your assets (good):

Computer equipment

Property

Goodwill

Stock

Debtors (how much your customers owe you including VAT)

Cash

All your liabilities (people you owe money to - bad)

Suppliers

Taxman (VAT, PAYE/NI (if you have employees), Corporation Tax (if you are a limited company)

Bank loans or overdrafts

Deferred Tax (should be a small number, you really don't need to know this one!)

Directors loan account (important – more on this later)

It then takes the liability number from the asset number and gives you a net asset figure. If this is a positive number (higher than 1), you are in business, if it is negative (less than 0), you are insolvent.

Secondly, it tells you your shareholder funds (this is right at the bottom). The shareholder funds should be exactly the same number as net assets. If it isn't call a 999 emergency accountant, your balance sheet is out of balance (which essentially means your whole accounts are out of wack!).

The shareholder funds is simply all the profits you have made EVER, less the amount you have taken out.

This is a crucial number to a bank to see if you are worth lending to. If you have made profits but rinsed the company, they won't like you. If you've left some in, they'll like you because they can use it as security. This goes against extracting your money in a tax efficient way, but if you want to raise funds you have to leave money in the business.

Thirdly, what the shareholder funds also tells you is that if your business closed today, the shareholders' funds would be the number that ends up in your bank account i.e. you would sell your computer equipment, sell your stock, collect all the money from your customers, pay your suppliers, pay the tax man and be left with a bank balance that will match shareholders' funds.

However, whilst accountants would say that the shareholders' funds is what your business is worth on *paper*, of course, your business is actually worth what someone is willing to pay for it.

Here's an example of a simple balance sheet:

Fixed assets

Computer equipment	£3,000
Furniture	£2,000

Current assets

Stock	£20,000

Debtors	£50,000
Cash	£10,000

Current liabilities	
Suppliers	-£20,000
PAYE/NI	-£5,000
VAT	-£15,000
Corporation Tax	-£10,000
Long term liabilities	
Bank loan	-£20,000
Deferred tax	-£1,000
Net assets	**£14,000**

Share capital	£1,000
Profit and loss account	£13,000
Shareholders' funds	**£14,000**

The most important numbers to keep your eye on are your Debtors, the customers who owe you money (including VAT), cash – the lifeblood of your business and that your liabilities don't exceed your assets.

I will talk about share capital in a later chapter.

What is a cash flow forecast?

A cash flow forecast should be for 13 weeks or 3 months. It can be for longer but simpler to start in a shorter period. 13 weeks is better than 3 months (i.e. 13 columns is better than 3) since a business can have some major cash fluctuations in a month.

Some key points about the cash flow:

Firstly, it is a guess! It is an educated guess, but it is a guess. The expenses should be reasonably straightforward to estimate because you know when you will physically pay them and they are in your control. The income from customers is harder because you don't know when your customers will pay you (although there are ways to make this more predictable).

Even though it is a guess, by doing the cash flow forecast you do get better at forecasting and I would say that every business should have one and try to forecast the cash.

Secondly, VAT is included on everything. It is trying to forecast physically what goes in and out of your bank account and that includes VAT.

Thirdly, VAT is the one number that can be the hardest to predict and the one number that will mess up your cash flow. PAYE/NI is every month and should be a consistent number. Corporation tax is once a year and your accountant should be able to tell you what this is way before you pay it. VAT is every quarter and can be variable so look out. It can kill your cash flow.

If you would like a very simple 13 week cash flow template email me at russell@rsaccountancy.co.uk.

The real power behind the cash flow forecast is that any business owner can handle a cash flow problem in 13 weeks. If your cash flow is saying you are going to run out of cash at the end of week 13, you've got lots of time to plan. Without knowing what's coming up, you could run out of cash by the end of next week (harder to deal with) or tomorrow (practically impossible – game over).

Why do a budget?

A business plan can be done at the start of your business or every new financial year or even every quarter. Many people ask me about what a business plan consists of and how they write it. Business owners can often over complicate a business plan but essentially a business plan is

"a bunch of numbers with some words justifying the numbers"

The 'bunch of numbers' is the budget. The numbers are a planned profit and loss account and cash flow forecast (you could include a balance sheet but personally I wouldn't bother unless you are raising finance and the plan is going to be read by a third party.

The gym I go to currently has a poster on the wall which reads "The worst work-out is one that doesn't get done". In the same way, it is better to try and do a budget then not to bother. Many people shy away from it because they think it is too hard and complicated. However, a budget is just a prediction of sales, profit and cash by the end of the year. Admittedly, cash is harder to predict than sales and profit but an accountant can help you do this.

Even if you don't want to pay an accountant to help you with your budget, just doing a 'back of a fag packet' calculation is better than not doing one at all, or not thinking about how the year in your business is going to pan out.

The other objection that some people have is:

"What's the point of doing a budget since I know things will change in my business?"

To which my response is, that this is the case in every business and the world in which we live in. Businesses are still able to budget effectively with enough practice and experience of knowing your business inside out. Even if your budget is completely wrong within a month. I remember Brian Tracy saying:

"The plan is useless but the planning is essential"

Often, just the discipline of sitting down to work out how the business is going to develop and progress in the year gives you tremendous insight into what the strengths and weaknesses of the business are. You will get insights that you would not have got without it.

So I would encourage you wholeheartedly to try and do even the most simple of budgets.

The real fun actually starts when you start comparing your actual sales, profit and cash to your budget. I could write a whole book on the discipline of tracking your numbers but for now I would encourage you to try it for a quarter and see the impact that it can have.

Tracking your numbers

Most business owners look at their numbers – sales, profit, cash – every month. However, I would argue that it is far better to look at the numbers every week. You can change things quicker and act accordingly. A month is a long time in business.

It does take a tremendous amount of discipline to review your numbers every week and you'll need a clear space in your diary (I do mine on Sunday evening, did I say I didn't have a life?) but it is worth it and it does increase your chances of hitting your targets.

Why do a forecast?

A forecast is quite simply a 're-budget'. Let us suppose you have written your budget at the start of the year. You have then documented the first month's results and compared them to your budget and realised that your budget is way out. A forecast is then 're-budgeting' the next eleven months in line with what you now know.

The forecast then replaces the original budget on a month by month basis as the numbers to go with. The budget remains in the background since at the end of the year you compare how well you actually budgeted (i.e. how close you were to reality). However, that really is all the budget is good for, the forecast becomes the living, breathing document.

The forecast can be redone as many times in the year as you want but you do want to avoid the situation where you have budgeted to make £100,000 profit and then with every month that goes by you drop the profit target by £10,000 (to end up on a loss of £20,000!). In an ideal world, the budgeted profit figure should remain the target profit throughout the year, the forecast is simply a different way to get to the same profit.

To avoid the huge disappointment of setting a high profit target to then miss it by miles in the first month (and then to ultimately crash out during the year under a weight of despair and disappointment) you must be REALISITC with your budget.

Having reviewed hundreds of budgets in my time as an accountant, the biggest problem isn't that the numbers don't add up, it is that the numbers are hugely inflated and bear no resemblance to what is realistic. This is mostly because a business owner, often by definition, will be filled with optimism about their great business. However, this optimism is hollow if you set a high profit target (and tell your team what this is), only for it to be way off the mark.

In my experience, it is better to set a realistic target and to just miss it, then to set a high target and to strive for it. Since in most cases, the majority of people will be so disappointed that they have begun to miss their target that they will end up doing worse.

You may have read the cliché:

"It is better to aim for the stars and to hit the moon than not to aim for the stars and hit nothing"

Well, essentially I'm saying this simply isn't the case for most people. It's better to aim for the moon and hit the moon.

You have probably heard of SMART goals (Smart, Measurable, Achievable, Realistic, Time-frame). The two words I get most questions on are: 'achievable' and 'realistic' – what is the difference?

If you were to ask me to run a marathon tomorrow, then it is possible that I may achieve this feat. Stranger things have happened, I am reasonably fit, it is not out of the bounds of possibility. However, if you knew that despite the fact that I can and do run (currently ranking 20th in the Fitbit accountants global league!), I have never run a marathon before and have done no preparation whatsoever. It is highly unlikely that I will be able to complete it.

In the same way, when you are assessing your profit and sales target, ask yourself the question: "Is this realistic? Do I know everything there is to know about hitting this profit and sales target?"

Again, if you have completed a budget that after the first month, it appears unrealistic, just re-forecast and move on. There is no point sticking to a budget that is not going to have any resemblance to reality.

Chapter 2 – Setting up your business

Introduction

When someone wants to start up their own business they are full of ideas of what products or services they will sell, where they will get work from and how they can take over the world. Sadly, many people are put off with the financial, legal and administration side of running a business.

This chapter is to essentially give you everything that you need to know about this side of starting a business. It isn't as complicated as people think although getting the business structure wrong at the beginning can have ramifications.

One of the biggest hurdles is the legal and financial jargon so I will try and de-code the jargon here.

Limited company vs self-employment – advantages and disadvantages

The word 'self-employment' is a generic term for anybody who works for themselves i.e. runs their own business. 'Their own business' can be in the form of a self-employed individual or a limited company.

There are a few types of limited company, the most common is a private limited company by shares which essentially means 'profit making'. Other non-profit making companies can be a limited company by guarantee or a community interest company. (If you are thinking of running a not-for-profit organisation, please bear in mind that any surplus in the year will be taxed, to avoid this you will have to become a charity).

On day one of a business, the choice for the business owner is either becoming a self-employed individual or a limited company.

There are three advantages of a limited company over self-employment and three disadvantages.

Advantage no. 1 – Protection from bankruptcy

If you become a limited company and your business goes bust, it is the company that goes bankrupt not yourself. This means that you can lose your business but not lose your house – very important! The reason this is possible is that in law, a 'limited company' means that all the business financial transactions are held in the limited company and are separate to the business owner. This is where the word 'limited' comes from. You are 'limited' in your liability.

The only way this doesn't happen is if you have given someone control over your personal assets i.e. you have raised money for your business from the bank but the bank has asked for a 'personal guarantee' i.e. something that overrides the limited company. In this way, if the business goes bankrupt, the bank comes after you.

Advantage no.2 – Commercial credibility

For some business owners, it will be important to appear bigger than they are. Being a limited company helps this (as does becoming VAT registered). This isn't always a vanity thing. In some industries, it is impossible to trade if you are not a limited company. For example, some local councils tend not to want to deal with self-employed individuals.

It is worth finding out whether becoming or not becoming a limited company actually matters to customers. For some, it will absolutely matter.

The reason why some customers want a limited company is that a limited company appears more official and legal than merely self-employment.

Advantage no. 3 – You save tax as a limited company

This is the best advantage and applies to every business with profits of over £30,000.

This is the current tax saving between a limited company and self-employment.

Profits	Tax saving
30,000	£498
40,000	£891
50,000	£1,423
60,000	£1,788
70,000	£1,456

You will need an accountant to make sure you get these tax savings (see disadvantages below), but there is a big tax saving for anybody thinking of becoming a limited company.

It all sounds good, but before you set up a limited company see below for the three disadvantages....

Disadvantage no. 1 – Accountancy fees are higher

Accountancy fees will be higher for a limited company than self-employment. This is because there is three times the level of work needed to run a limited company. Although on profit levels of £30,000 and above, your tax savings will more than cover this.

Also, as a limited company, you will need an accountant.

Some self-employed individuals successfully compete their tax returns themselves. As a limited company, you will need to get an accountant since the limited company accounts are far more complicated than a tax return.

Here is a run-down of what an accountant will do for you if you are a self-employed individual or a limited company.

Self employed

Personal Tax return
Simple accounts (optional)

Limited company

Personal tax return
Director's payroll
Full statutory limited company accounts for HM Revenue & Customs
Abbreviated statutory limited company accounts for Companies House
Corporation tax return
Annual return

Disadvantage no. 2 – You need a company bank account

It is possible to run your self-employed business through your own personal current account and thus avoid extra bank charges and the hassle of setting up another bank account.

If you are a limited company, you will need to set up a company bank account and the bank will charge you (although you can get offers of free banking for the first year or two)

Disadvantage no. 3 – There is more to do and think about as a limited company

As you can see above, there is more going on with running a limited company and whilst an accountant will do most of it for you, there are more things to be aware of and learn.

The relationship with your accountant is likely to be more involved and communication more regular as well.

If you are starting a business then self-employment is often the most straight-forward option since it is the easiest to set up (see below). You can also change from self-employment to limited company at any point (although slightly messier to change the other way round).

What are umbrella companies?

There is a third option that some businesses choose and this is an umbrella company. It is sort of a cross between self-employed and running a limited company.

Essentially, it is a limited company that is run for you by someone else (a third party that runs umbrella companies). If you are a contractor caught by IR35 (more on this later), umbrella companies are a straightforward way of operating.

Register for self-employment

If you opt for self-employment then the first step, registering, is very very easy.

Call this number: 0300 200 3504. This is the HMRC helpline for the newly self-employed.

They will ask you for a few details, name, address etc.

When the registration process is complete, you will be given a new code, the UTR – unique tax reference (this is in addition to your national insurance (NI) number.

Paying Class 2 National Insurance

The first thing that will happen (unfortunately) is that you will begin to pay something that you have never paid before – Class 2 National Insurance. This is the national insurance contributions for people who are self-employed (you probably have been used to paying Class 1 as an employee). It is currently £3.00 a week and is paid annually with the other tax on the personal tax return.

If you are self-employed and employed at the same time, you want to opt out of this since there is no need to pay Class 1 and Class 2.

You can also opt out of Class 2 if you think your profits will be lower than £6,365 but I don't recommend it.

Bank account for self employed

As much as your bank will want you to run your self-employment through a business bank account, there really is no need. I would recommend setting up a different account to your normal personal account as this will make running your accounts far easier.

Share structures for a limited company

A self-employed individual is just a person with a business, a limited company is a separate business organisation to the business owner. It is a (jargon alert) legal entity that means the business owner is protected from its results (unless you commit fraud, you can still be prosecuted as an unscrupulous director).

Every limited company has shareholders, directors and employees.

For example, in a 1 person limited company, the business owner will be all three. They will be a shareholder because they own shares in the company (typically 1 share out of a possible 1 i.e. 100%). A shareholder is there to collect profits. If the business makes a profit, the shareholder can take profit out of the business (after tax). The shareholder doesn't have to do anything other than to collect money (great job!).

In much larger businesses, the shareholders have done something significant, which is invest money in the business. They are then paid for the risk that they have taken. The best way to think about this is using the example of 'Dragons Den'. In this TV program, investors out bid each other to invest in a start-up business. The business owner will want cash to grow their business, the 'Dragon' (Investor) wants to invest cash but in return they want a 'stake' in the business, e.g. 20%, 40%, 50%.

If the business owner agrees, this means that the Dragon can basically collect money for ever in return of putting in the money at the beginning. Of course, in Dragon Den's case, it is unlikely that the Dragon will be a silent shareholder. Because of their experience they will want to be involved to ensure that they do get a return of their money, but technically they don't have to.

Another example is if somebody has shares in a large organisation like ASDA. In this case, the shareholder will really do nothing at all other than to hope they get a pay-out (dividend) every year.

For a one person limited company, the shareholder will be doing all the work since it is their own business and nobody else will do it. But technically speaking, the shareholder is only there to recoup profits after their initial investment.

The one person business owner will also be a director. It is directors that run the company. The director is technically an employee as well (even if they don't actually get any money for it). In the most efficient tax saving structure, the 1 person business owner will get paid as a shareholder (dividends) and as an employee (salary).

Do these distinctions really matter in a one person company?

Probably not. Where it really matters is if there are two or more people in the business.

So for example, if you set up a business and want to bring your partner into it (be they a wife, husband or business partner), you really must know what they are coming into the business as.

If they are a shareholder and you decide to give them half of the shares, this means that you and your partner own 50% each of the shares. The company is no longer your own and you don't have majority stake in your business. So you have to choose wisely before you do this and I would always advise getting a shareholders agreement to ensure any problems in the future are dealt with fairly and with clarity. You may be friends now with no money but let's see how you get on with money and success (have you seen 'The Social Network'?).

A 50/50 limited company where two people are running it are likely to be both shareholders and directors. However, if you are bringing in a second person to your business as more of a 'key employee' rather than a 'partner', then you would not want to make them a shareholder, you would make them an employee. If they ask for shares, think very carefully if you want to give up some of your company. To me, this is as serious as getting married, in that you could be stuck with this person for many years to come and having worked on shareholder disputes for years, I can tell you horror stories of how things can go wrong.

Having said that, some shareholder partnerships work amazingly well. All I would advise is, proceed with caution and get a shareholder agreement.

What if I want to bring my spouse into the business?

Bringing a spouse into the business as either an employee or director can be a very effective tax saving tip. Again, remember that you are potentially giving away 50% of your business. Having said this, I am a massive fan of splitting businesses for tax reasons since the tax savings can be huge and if you are worried about sharing your business, the lawyers I've spoken to say that your spouse would get half of it anyway if you split up so what does it matter? (That's not legal advice by the way – if you are worried speak to a lawyer).

If you are in relationship with someone and not married – what are you waiting for? There are huge tax benefits of getting married, you could be losing thousands in tax just because you don't tie the knot. Proponents of living together always say that marriage is 'just a piece of paper'. This isn't the case for tax purposes.

Whilst I have continued to tell my clients to get married for tax reasons, to date, I'm not sure any of them have heeded my advice. Oh well, I'll keep trying!

In conclusion, you will have to answer most of these questions before you set up the company so it is worth thinking about now. You can change share structures one the company is set up but it can be a bit messy and could cost you tax.

So what else do you need to set up the company?

Companies can be set up within 24 hours, you just need:

Company Name
Registered Office
Director name, address, occupation, nationality and date of birth
Share %

Usually, the company name you have thought up will be available (it will be so good/bad that nobody would have thought of it before). If it isn't available, a small variation of it is fine. Your actual limited company name doesn't have to be your trading name. So even if your trading name is taken as a company name, it doesn't necessarily mean you can't use it (unless you want to call yourself McDonalds or Marks & Spencer).

Once the company is set up, you then need to…

Set up a company bank account. You may think this is a straightforward process but I always tell clients to allow for 2-4 weeks for the bank to get their act together. It is often quicker if you set up with the bank you bank personally with, although some clients are not keen for their bank to know all their finances. You will need your incorporation certificate to give a copy to the bank (a one page document with your new company number on).

Corporation Tax office

Once the company is set up at Companies House, they will then inform the tax office that a new company has been set up. In approximately, three weeks you will get a form from the Corporation Tax office, 'Notice of a new company'. This form will ask you when you are trading from. You can set up a limited company and not actually trade through it to begin with. Usually though limited companies will trade from the beginning.

Once this form is sent off, you will be registered with the Corporation Tax office and officially active as a limited company.

Self-assessment

As well as completing abbreviated accounts for Companies House and full accounts and a Corporation Tax return for the Corporation Tax office, you also have to complete a personal tax return.

If you are already completing a personal tax return because you are a higher rate employee or you own property or have other income, you don't then need to do anything. If however, you have never completed a personal tax return, you need to register to complete one.

Should you become VAT registered?

The rules for VAT registration are the same for self-employed people as well as limited companies.

The basic rule is if your sales are going to be more than £85,000 in the next 12 months you should register for VAT.

You can still register for VAT even if your sales don't go above £85,000. The reason why you may do this is to appear to customers bigger than you are.

If you want to become VAT registered, read Chapter 4 where I will go through the four different types of VAT method there are.

Should I become registered for VAT MOSS?

From 1 January 2015, a new VAT rule came in which so far has had profound implications on how to account for VAT. It affects 1 million businesses across the EU.

If you want to know whether your business will be caught by the VAT MOSS rules, follow the questions below…

1. Do you sell to the EU?

2. Do you sell digital products (no or minimal human intervention)?

3. Do you sell business to consumer in the EU (if you sell to a 'marketplace' this could be 'business to business' and therefore MOSS doesn't apply)

If the answer is yes to all three, you have to:

a) Register
b) Complete VAT MOSS returns
c) Account for the VAT on the country of the customer (not UK VAT)

Important: All this applies whether or not you are registered for VAT in the UK

This is a new and tricky area, if you need further help on this, email me at russell@rsaccountancy.co.uk

IR35

If you are a one person limited company and you only do work for one customer, it is possible that you will be caught by the IR35 rules.

These rules were introduced to eradicate the tax benefits of an employee setting up as a limited company and then working for the previous employer.

It is important to be able to prove that you are indeed self-employed rather than employed in case HMRC investigate you and seek to apply the IR35 rules. These rules were designed to catch contractors who had left employment and were working for the same company as self-employed.

If HMRC were able to prove that you fall under the IR35 rules then they would seek to tax you as an employee rather than self-employed.

So it is important to ensure you don't fall under IR35. HMRC look at the whole picture of your relationship with your employer/client but here are some of the ways to mitigate being caught by IR35.

1. You have to act like a business rather than an employee e.g. send invoices to the client, have your own stationery, use your own equipment but most crucially of all have other revenue streams/clients so that you are not working for one company

2. If your contract can be interpreted as the client having control over you then this would suggest the client has authority over your working habit and could put you within IR35. For example, ideally you wouldn't have the client giving you specified working hours, specific working days and break times

3. Working at a client's premises doesn't normally risk IR35 but it is important to state that this might happen and for what reason

4. A contract safe from IR35 should not have promises from the client of regular, ongoing work. The contract should state when

the contractor will invoice and what the terms on the invoice will be.

5. Contractors do not benefit from sick pay, pensions, holiday pay, paternity pay or any other rights than an employee can be entitled to

Since 1 March 2017, HMRC released a very useful questionnaire to work out whether you are caught by IR35. You can find it here:

https://www.tax.service.gov.uk/check-employment-status-for-tax/setup

Since 1 April 2017, the government has made public organisations responsible for determining whether their workers are caught by IR35. Some of these organisations have decided to blanket everyone under IR35 (whether they are or not). If this happens to you, it is worth completing the questionnaire and if you are not caught by IR35, showing this to your client (or agency) and arguing your case.

At the time of writing, the IR35 situation is fast-moving and confusing for many contractors, if you need more help me at russell@rsaccountancy.co.uk.

Chapter 3 – Pricing and your day rate

Introduction

Arriving at your prices is one of the hardest things in business. It is particularly difficult when you first start your business since you may not have a good understanding of your market or what other people charge. Also, when you start a business you may just be grateful that someone is paying you *anything* let alone a price that you are worth.

It's worth putting in the groundwork to think about what you will charge since your price says so much about your business and your service. The price you start with is very important as people will come to you based on word of mouth referrals so they will have an understanding of what their friends have paid. It is possible to increase your prices over the cycle of your business but it is harder if you are starting from a low base.

Here are some tips to help you think about what your pricing should be.

Tips on pricing

1. Do as much research in your market as possible. When I started my business, I got my sister-in-law to phone up as many accountancy firms as she could to get an understanding of what the range of prices were (this was much harder than it sounds as accountants are a shy bunch and often were not able to give quotes over the phone).

2. Speak to anybody you know who is doing the same work as you, find out what they charge. If you don't know anybody, join an organisation of fellow businesses, you'll be surprised at how open people will be.

3. Decide on what your price strategy will be. This is something that very few businesses do. What most businesses do is to carry out the above two tips and then pitch themselves at the average of what everyone else is charging. Result: an average business. I often see businesses advertise 'great services at competitive prices'. This is highly difficult to pull off. Amazon may have done it (although not for Lego!) but unless you are as ambitious or skilled as Jeff Bezos I wouldn't even try. Focus on great service OR great prices OR great product. Don't try to be everything, it is virtually impossible.

4. Think twice about being the cheapest. First of all, price is one of the top 5 factors why people buy but only in 20% of cases is it the most important. It takes a certain personality who wants the cheapest and simply put, these aren't much fun to be around.

5. Know what you are really worth to the market. If you are coming from a well-paid job, then you probably have a good idea of what you are worth. If you are launching a business to increase your earning power then you may not know as well. Concentrate on what value you are bringing to the market place, truly understand what you are selling to people. At RS Accountancy, we DO accounts, tax returns and VAT returns, but what we are actually giving to people is peace of mind, protection from HMRC and the opportunity to save tax.

6. Understand that people buy from people. Unless you have created something that is truly unique that nobody else is selling, the chances of you having a USP (Unique Sales Proposition) is slim. In fact, your USP is yourself. There is nobody like you and if you do a good job and people like you then that is what you will build your reputation on.

Working out the maths of your day rate

If you are a service business then you will either offer a fixed fee, an hourly rate or a day rate.

It is at this point where you need a bit of maths to make the correct decision on your pricing (bear with me).

Let's say you are paid at your current employment a salary of £40,000. There are 1,950 hours in the year (52 x 37.5 hours). Therefore £40,000 divided by 1,950 is £20.51 per hour. So this should be your hourly rate, right? Wrong!

Your employment covers lots of things that your self-employment will not.

For example, your current employer pays you £40,000 not to do 1,950 of *chargeable* work i.e work that can be charged to the client. Here's what they have to pay for:

-   Holiday
-   Sick pay
-   Pension
-   Training
-   Appraisal
-   Toilet breaks
-   Cigarette breaks (well, maybe)
-   Sorting out your desk
-   The times when you were mucking about

AND they have to pay National Insurance at 13.8% on top of your £40,000 which calculates at approximately £4,500. So they actually pay you £44,500 for all of these things.

Your future clients will not pay you for any of these, not the holidays, not the sick pay, not for you to muck about!

So your day rate has to incorporate all of this otherwise, you'll do 1,950 hours in your self-employment but you will be working harder and earning less.

If you take into account your holiday which let's say is 22 days + 8 days statutory, this equates to approximately a month of being paid to sit on the beach. Therefore, if you still want to have a holiday in your self-employment, you'll need to increase the £20.51 by AT LEAST 9% (12 divided by 11) but in reality, £21.82 isn't going to cut it.

You've probably heard that your friends who are self-employed earn more than you do. Their hourly rates may be much higher than yours. However, remember that they don't get any of the benefits of being employed and they don't get the biggest benefit not mentioned above which is STEADY JOB. Yes, it is true that you could lose your job, but when you are self-employed you are living from one client to the next, one project to the next. It is your responsibility to find work, whilst being employed usually you are given work.

All of this must be included in your hourly rate. If you have wondered why self-employed people get paid more it is because they are WORTH IT. How I do know? Because someone has deemed them valuable enough to pay them.

Charging out your employees or freelancers

I write about taking on employees or freelancers in a later chapter. However, for now, let's cover how much you should charge your employees or freelancers out at.

The common ratio is to charge a day rate or hourly rate at 3 times what you pay them. A third of this covers their payment, a third of this covers the overheads of your business and a third should be profit. This is a very traditional ratio and different industries will have different ratios but whatever you do, you need to make sure you are making profits out of your employees.

Bizarrely, some people in business appear to have a bit of a problem with this idea. They either feel guilty for making money out of their team OR they are worried that their team may just go off and steal their clients.

Firstly, don't feel guilty. If you don't make profits then you don't have a business (see the first chapter). If you don't have a business then you aren't able to employ anybody. Secondly, it is very rare for your team to think about stealing your clients. Most people have morals and ethics AND if they see how hard you work running your own business they will want to run a mile. They just want to do the work.

So whether you charge them out at 3 times or 10 times, make sure you do make profits out of your team for the good of your business.

Fixed fees vs hourly rates

This can be a very tricky decision. I was charging fixed fees back in the day when the vast majority of accountants were charging hourly fees. I was attracted to fixed fees because they were so much more appealing to clients and much easier to sell. However, you live and die by fixed fees. If you charge an amount and you do the job much quicker than you anticipated then great! If you get the fixed fee wrong and the job takes ages – then....oh dear!

Your industry will have people who charge fixed fees or hourly rates and you'll have to decide what works for you. In both cases, you will need to get the price right and the more work you do, the better you will become at quoting.

If you need more help on pricing feel free to email me at russell@rsaccountancy.co.uk

Chapter 4 – Sales Invoices

What goes on a sales invoice

Here's a list of what you should put on a sales invoice….

A Sales invoices should include the following:

a) The name of your business at the top
b) The name of your customer at the top
c) Date
d) Invoice number
e) Amount
f) Detailed description of the service given
g) Payment terms
h) Telephone number to contact for any problems with the invoice

Do not put VAT on your invoice unless you are VAT registered. You don't have to become VAT registered until your sales reach £85,000 in one year).

If it is your first business, start the numbers at a random four digit number (so not to tell the world it is your first piece of work!).

If you are a limited company, you must also put your registered office and company number.

Chapter 5 – Claiming expenses

Claiming expenses: what does it mean?

One of the most common questions I get asked, is 'what expenses can I claim?'

Before I answer this, let's understand what claiming expenses doesn't mean.

If you incur a cost in your business, for example a £100 train ticket, you will be able to claim this as an expense of your business. This does not mean, however, that the full cost of the train ticket is paid back to you by HMRC ! It is not the same as claiming expenses as an employee to an employer where they would pay you the whole amount back.

Here's how it actually works…..

Here's your profit and loss account in a limited company (though the same principle applies in self employment)

Sales	£10,000
Costs	-£4,000
Profit	£6,000
Tax @ 19%	-£1,140

Notice when we put the £100 train ticket in to the 'costs' in the accounts

Sales	£10,000
Costs	-£4,100
Profit	£5,900
Tax @ 19%	-£1,121

The cost goes up by £100, the profit goes down by £100, the tax goes down by £19 – 19%

So because we have claimed the £100 train ticket against the income, our tax has gone down by £19.

If you wanted to know how much the train ticket was actually costing you, then it would be £81 (£100 less the £19 tax saving).

It will never cost you nothing! HMRC are not going to reimburse you for the £100 train ticket they are only going to allow it as a tax deductible expense which means that in the tax calculation, the cost goes against income and therefore reduces the profit and therefore the tax.

So there are two key points to draw from this:

Point no. 1 – If you miss out costs in your accounts (which is easily done – think of the train ticket getting lost or not being recorded), you will pay more tax than you need to, since your profit is artificially high.

Point no. 2 – if you are thinking about investing in marketing, training course, employee, computer or piece of equipment, remember that if the cost is £1,000, it will always actually cost you 19% less i.e. £810 because the tax will be reduced by £190

Note. If you are self-employed, the tax is usually reduced by 29% and if you are VAT registered, you can reduce the cost by a further 20% because you can claim the VAT back (as long as you are not on the flat rate VAT scheme.

What expenses can I claim?

So getting back to the original question, here is a summary of the expenses that you can claim in your business (it applies to limited companies and self-employment). This list is not exhaustive, so if you want to check another expense that is not in this list feel free to email me on russell@rsaccountancy.co.uk.

Cost of sales
Raw Materials

Stock
Other direct costs e.g. packing/despatch
Freelancers

Overheads

Employee costs (this could also be in cost of sales if a service business)
Salaries, wages, bonuses, Employers NI, pension contributions, casual wages, canteen costs, recruitment agency fees, subcontractors and other wages costs

Premises costs
Rent, ground rent, rates, water, refuse, light and heat, property, insurance, security and use of home

Repairs
Repair of property, replacements, renewals, maintenance

General administrative expenses
Telephone, fax, mobile telephone, stationery, photocopying, printing, postage, courier and computer costs, subscriptions and insurance

Motoring expenses
Petrol, servicing, licence, repairs, motor insurance, hire and leasing, car parking, RAC/AA membership

Travel and subsistence
Rail, air, bus, travel, taxis subsistence and hotel costs

Entertainment
Staff entertaining (e.g. Christmas party), customer gifts up to £50 per person advertising your business

Advertising and promotion
Advertising, promotion, mailshots, free samples, brochures, newsletters, trade shows

Legal and professional costs
Accountancy, legal, architects, surveyors, stocktakers' fees, indemnity insurance

Bad debts

Interest On bank loans, overdraft and other loans

Other finance charges
Bank charges, HP interest, credit card charges, leasing not already included

Depreciation and losses on sale

NOT ALLOWED: Customer entertaining, Food if not away from home (e.g. 40 miles from home)

What expenses can't I claim?

The general rule is that an expense can be claimed if it is 'wholly, necessarily and exclusively for business'. So if you have a cost that you wouldn't have spent money on if you were not running a business, then it is likely not to be tax deductible.

The three most common expenses that people think can be claimed are as follows:

a) Customer entertaining

I think it is because people have seen business people in the city having drinks at bars or food in restaurants with customers and thought that all of this was perfectly legitimate business expenditure. Whilst the employee will claim back any personal expenditure from the employer (reimbursement of expenses), when the accountants look at the corporation tax return (for the company), they will disallow all entertaining.

The truth is that customer entertaining is never, ever, ever, ever tax deductible. It can be a perfectly legitimate business expenditure (and one that I encourage since it can end up being cheap marketing expenditure for big results) but it is not tax deductible. This means that it will happily sit in the profit and loss account as a cost but when the company tax return is done, it is ignored.

There is some entertaining that is tax deductible and that is employee entertaining. You can claim employee entertaining up to £150 per employee per year. There are also some reliefs available for award voucher schemes that you set up (e.g. best sales person of the month etc.)

b) Food

Food is never, ever, ever, ever, ever tax deductible UNLESS you are away from home on business. I define 'away from home' as 40 miles. However, there really is no HMRC definition to 'away from home' so you have to use common sense. If you are staying over somewhere then the food is allowable but you don't have to stay over to claim food.

There are also limits to how much you can claim, preventing you from living it up every time you leave home on business (although remember it is your own money that you are spending, you will only claim back 20% / 29% of the cost through the accounts.

This is a tricky area and it depends on a case by case basis. If you want further clarification, email me at russell@rsaccountancy.co.uk.

In the meantime, have a look at the following list of questions to see where the cost fits in:

You spend food in your business:

Is it entertaining staff?

YES – Tax deductible (up to £150 per employee per year)

NO…………….

Is it entertaining clients/customers?

YES – Legitimate business expense for the accounts but not tax deductible, needs to be added back on Corporation Tax return (disallowed)

NO…………………

Is it subsistence? (i.e. food consumed on a business trip more than 40 miles from home)

YES – Tax deductible

NO – Directors loan account (paid for by the business but the director has to reimburse the company as it is a personal cost)

c) Fines

Any fines that are not tax deductible, e.g. parking fines, speeding fines, HMRC fines, Companies House fines.

d) Tax

Tax is not in itself tax deductible. You always get taxed on profits which is after all the expenditure (see Chapter 1). To make it slightly confusing, the tax that you pay on behalf of your employees (their PAYE tax and Employees National Insurance) and the tax that you pay on top of employees' salaries (Employers National Insurance) is tax deductible in the accounts.

Costs that are a mixture of business and personal

There are some costs in your business that will be both business and personal such as:

a) Mobile and landline telephone bills

I certainly wouldn't encourage you to get two mobiles. Simply get itemised billing and have a decent stab at estimating what % is business. I wouldn't do this every month (you won't have time) but maybe do it twice a year and err on the side of caution i.e. don't over-cook it!

It is also a good idea to record in the supplementary information box on the self-employment page your % estimates, it is often better to disclose more information to HMRC than less.

b) Cars

I'm often asked whether it is better to put their car in the business or leave it in the business owner's own name. At my firm, we regularly take this question on for clients but it does end up with hugely complicated calculations with some hair raising results i.e. getting this decision wrong can cost you £3,000 of extra tax or more.

However, the chances are that it is better to keep your car in your personal name from a tax perspective. This is because the government hates cars, especially nice cars (i.e. big cars with large CO_2 emissions) and so ramped up the tax bills for directors with company cars. Although having a nice car doesn't always mean high CO_2 emissions (if you watch 'Top Gear' you'll know what I'm talking about, please note – I don't watch 'Top Gear', I'm not that sort of guy!).

Feel free to email me at russell@rsaccountancy.co.uk if you want a specific answer but if you want a quick, simple, easy and low-hassle answer, then:

1. Keep your car in your personal name

2. Record the amount of business miles you travel in a notebook every week

3. At the end of the year, add up your miles and multiply it by 45p – this is the cost of your motor travel

4. It drops down to 25p after the first 10,000 miles (on every mile over 10,000)

5. You don't need to keep petrol receipts and all other motor costs (e.g. insurance, road tax, repairs) are irrelevant.

Please note: Vans are a different thing entirely, the tax rates are much more generous. Generally, it is better for your van to be in your business.

c) Home costs

It is likely that you do some work at home and are incurring some extra cost in doing this (at the very least, heat, light and electricity).

There are two ways to do this.

The simpler way is to charge your business £208 per year (this is £4 a week). This is the minimal amount you can put through the business without HMRC asking any questions. However, it isn't much and will only save you about £41.60 tax in a company and £60.32 in self-employment.

If you think your home costs are more than this, then I do have a useful spreadsheet that you can use to work this out. Please email me at russell@rsaccountancy.co.uk for a copy.

Capital items

Jargon alert! Capital means assets which means any big cost! For example, a computer is a cost that doesn't go through the profit and loss account in one go. This is because, accounting rules dictate that the computer will last the business for more than one year (probably three years). So, we put the computer on the balance sheet as an asset and depreciate it (write it off) to the profit and loss account over three years.

So for example if you purchase a computer for £1,200. Then the profit and loss account will show £400 in the first year, £400 in the second year and £400 in the third year. At the end of the third year, neither the profit and loss account or the balance sheet will show any trace of the computer since it is now worth zero (even if you are still using it).

Whilst this is interesting from an accounts point of view, the way the tax works is completely different. The tax rules write the whole computer off in one year. So if you purchase the computer you will get the full tax deduction (19% of £1,200) in the first year.

The way that it is actually recorded on the tax return is slightly different, it goes in the 'capital allowance' box rather than as a normal expense, the effect is the same calling into question whether you even needed to read this chapter (or whether I even needed to write it!).

Pre business expenses

It is often the case that you will have some costs associated with the business before you've actually set up your limited company or set up your self-employment.

You should definitely keep all your receipts and paperwork since this can be brought into your accounts at day one of the business starting.

The only slight complication for a limited company is that effectively the director has paid for them on the company's behalf so needs to be reimbursed.

Charging your client or customer expenses

This is an interesting area which many clients get wrong.

Let's suppose you are a service business and you do some work for a client which you will charge £1,000 for. However, to do the work, you have to go to the client's premises and therefore incur travel expenses.

You agree with the client that you will charge 45p per mile and it is a round trip of 20 miles - £9. You also have to stay in a hotel which costs you £50, which again, the client agrees to pay.

Your invoice looks like this:

Service	£1,000
Travel	£9
Hotel	£50
Total	£1,059

So far so good.

However, make sure that you also include the travel cost in your expenses as well as your sales invoice.

The profit on this job should be £1,000 i.e. you've charged your client £59 but incurred £59 of cost which nets off.

If you forget to include the £9 in your costs, you will effectively be paying tax on the £1,059.

If you are VAT registered, there is something else to know which catches out even more people.

If you are a VAT registered, your invoice should look like this:

Service	£1,000
Travel	£9
Hotel	£50
Net	£1,059
VAT @ 20%	£211.80
Gross	£1,270.80

Notice that I have charged 20% VAT on the total cost. Wait, you'll say, doesn't the travel already have VAT included, therefore shouldn't it be split out.

You would think! But you would be wrong. Yes, you say, but you are charging VAT on VAT. You are correct but as the great Punch once said 'that's the way to do it'.

I appreciate that it makes no sense but that's the rules!

I've actually had my clients' customers ask for invoices to be changed and on a couple of occasions spoken to my clients' customers directly.

(If you are not VAT registered you don't need to deal with the above madness!).

Chapter 6 – Keeping good records

Introduction

Part of running a business is to keep good records. There are a couple of reasons to do this:

    a)   Being organised

If you are not generally an organised person, then you want to either get organised or get someone in your team who is. Running the multiple disciplines of a business: customer service, selling, marketing, delivering the service, financial control, team management, time management, calendar management, requires a very high degree of organisation.

If you can get your financials and financial paperwork organised then this will give you a solid base. A great accountant will help you on this, but they won't do everything for you.

If you really do worry about this, a good bookkeeper or PA could help you.

    b)   HMRC

As part of our service to clients we always include a 'tax investigation' service, which effectively means that if a client is investigated by HMRC we will do all the work needed for free no matter how long it takes.

I'm often asked what is the likelihood of being investigated by HMRC? In order to answer this, I once read a very long tax manual that went through all the criteria of how HMRC chooses who to investigate (I did this whilst you were out having a life). My conclusion was that it appeared very random.

If you are in business for the next 30 years, the certainty I can give is that it is bound to happen at least once, if not many times. You also have to keep all records for seven years.

All records can be kept digitally except for dividend vouchers and notes of directors meetings (see later on) which must be kept in paper form.

So what are good records?

Here is a run-down of all the records that you have to keep:

- Sales invoices
- Purchase invoices from suppliers
- Any other expenses or receipts
- Bank statements
- Paying in books and cheque stubs
- HMRC correspondence
- Companies House correspondence
- Record of paying employees
- VAT returns (if you are VAT registered)

If you need a template of a sales invoice please email me at russell@rsaccountancy.co.uk

What is bookkeeping and who should do it?

Bookkeeping is the recording of all the financial transactions in your business (it is also the only word in the English language with a triple double i.e. two of the same letters in a row three times!).

Every business needs regular bookkeeping, the questions are: Who does the bookkeeping? What do they do? How do they do it?

Who does the bookkeeping?

Like lots of things when you first start a business and when you continue to grow a business, you have to decide what your time is worth as the business owner. Once you've decided what your time is worth you then have to decide what business tasks you will do yourself and tasks that you will outsource i.e. pay someone else to do.

A quick note on outsourcing. Successful leveraging time by outsourcing is one of the keys to successful business growth. But one thing I have learnt to my detriment is that you can't just find a supplier, pay them some money and tell them to get on with it. Successful outsourcing means treating the supplier like a team member, managing them, checking up on them, being clear in your communication about what you want. If you can master outsourcing, you are well on your way to business success.

One of the immediate tasks as soon as you start the business is who does the bookkeeping? Your choices are, do it yourself, pay a bookkeeper to do it or pay an accountant to do it.

The advantages of doing it yourself are firstly, you don't pay someone else. Keeping costs low at the beginning of your business is essential as you work out what you are doing. This way if you make lots of mistakes, you'll keep the financial costs of those mistakes to a minimum. Secondly, you get a chance to get your hands dirty and really understand what is going on in the business. Again, this can be essential in the early days, knowing what money is coming in and what money is going out.

The disadvantages are quite simply doing something that will take you away from making money and growing the business. Whilst not doing bookkeeping can lead to financial ruin, there are plenty of people who can do it for you.

I've met business owners who do everything themselves to keep costs down, but then are unable to grow the business because there isn't enough time in the day. I've also met people who outsource everything but then don't manage their suppliers, don't have a firm grip on what they are paying out and in some cases, don't actually seem to be doing much work themselves.

The trick is to strike the balance and the balance is about timing i.e. you do outsource but you do it at the right time. I remember a client and friend of mine (who was a very successful business owner – becoming a millionaire by selling his start up) saying to me 'I know how to do everything in my business'. Of course, he didn't do everything in his business (his business had 80 employees) but he knew how to do everything.

Having said all that, if you really are terrible at numbers and have no aptitude for maths, then it really is pointless trying to do the bookkeeping. It won't be in your flow, you'll do it badly, and you'll resent the time taken when you could be doing something you enjoy and that is more productive for the business (I would encourage you to keep reading this chapter though, since you need to know about finances even if you don't do them yourself).

If you decide to outsource the bookkeeping, there are two options. Firstly, to hire a bookkeeper and secondly to ask your accountant to do it.

A bookkeeper will come to your office every month or quarter and be a bit more hands on. Asking you lots of questions, setting up a bookkeeping system in your business. Like everything, there are good and bad bookkeepers. A good bookkeeper will be someone who doesn't just passively enter information into a computer, they will get a grip on the business finances, be a pain in the neck to you by ensuring you don't lose receipts and record your expenditure. Good bookkeepers are hard to find but I do know many good ones if you would like to email me on russell@rsaccountancy.co.uk I can send you details.

Accountants can do the bookkeeping as well, either monthly or quarterly. Accountants generally have higher hourly rates than bookkeepers although it depends on how they do the bookkeeping whether or not it actually costs more. Often, the relationship with the accountant on the bookkeeping side will be a little more distant than having a bookkeeper come into your premises (although some accountants will come to your premises as well).

What does the bookkeeper do?

In summary, this is what the bookkeeper does:

Step 1 - Invoices

- Raise the sales invoices
- Record the sales invoices in the accounts (both the sale and the debt owed FROM the customer)
- Give the purchase invoice / expense receipt a reference number
- Record the purchase invoices in the accounts (both the expenditure and the debt owed TO the supplier)

Step 2 – Payments and receipts

- Record the customer receipt (both the bank receipt and the clearing of the customer debt)
- Record the supplier payment (both the bank payment and the payment of the supplier debt)

Step 3 – Reconcile the bank to the accounts

- Go through all the bank receipts and bank payments in the account and tick this off against the bank account (this is called the bank reconciliation)

Step 4 – Review list of customers and suppliers

- Go through the list of customers who owe money to ensure they are correct
- Go through the list of suppliers who you owe money to ensure they are correct

Step 5 – Review your profit and loss account and balance sheet for any errors

Step 6 – (If VAT registered) complete the VAT returns

How do they do the bookkeeping?

Simple answer – on software. I do have some clients who still do their accounts manually but that is very uncommon.

If you are starting a business and you think that your turnover (sales) will be under £100,000 and you don't have lots of transactions then I would recommend a simple Excel spreadsheet.

If you would like this spreadsheet for free, email me at russell@rsaccountancy.co.uk.

For bigger businesses there are lots of types of accounting software.

These are split into the cloud based software (i.e. software you access online) and the desktop based software.

Here are some examples of the cloud based software:

Xero

FreeAgent

Kashflow

Sage ONE

Quickbooks online

Pandle

Here are some examples of desktop based software:

VT

Sage

Quickbooks

In my accountancy firm, we have clients who use all of these software packages so I am used to all of them.

Here are my current recommendations. On the cloud based software side, I think that Xero and FreeAgent are the ones that clients like the most with FreeAgent probably edging it.

(Full disclosure: we do actually offer FreeAgent at a discounted rate).

On the desktop based software, Sage is far too big for a smaller business, VT is very quick to use but doesn't have as pretty an interface as the others and Quickbooks is somewhere in between.

Picking a software package that can import the bank balance is a good idea as this will save you lots of time (most of the cloud packages can do this). Alas, as much as I love VT, it cannot do this!

VAT

The accounts of a business step up in complexity once the business becomes VAT registered.

You don't need to become VAT registered until your sales reach the £85,000 mark.

Becoming VAT registered for a business can be quite a daunting task and psychologically a bit of a barrier to growth.

The advantage of becoming VAT registered is that you can now claim back VAT on your expenditure. The disadvantage is that you have to charge VAT on your sales. This means that if you were charging your customer £1,000 for a service, you now have to charge them £1,200 (VAT is 20% = £200). The customer doesn't benefit from this, they now pay £200 extra for nothing and you don't benefit since all you do is pay the £200 over to HMRC.

If your customer base are VAT registered (i.e. businesses bigger than £83,000 turnover) then they won't mind being charged VAT since they just claim the VAT against their own VAT on their own sales – no big deal. However, if your customers are not VAT registered, then you have just increased your prices by 20% and your customer receives nothing extra for this and neither do you.

I'm often asked if there is any way around this and the answer is pretty much 'no'.

I've seen people set up different limited companies for different services they offer to avoid going over the VAT threshold but personally I think this is unnecessarily complicated. If you want to run a business that is lower than £85,000 then that is up to you, but if you want to make some real money and grow something great then you will need to accept that you'll have to become VAT registered.

If you do then become VAT registered and you know that the customer cannot recover the VAT that you will charge them, you have a choice of whether to absorb the VAT yourself, charge 100% of the VAT to the customer or somewhere in between.

My advice is to be very careful.

If you were charging £1,000 to a customer and are now charging £1,200, your customer may baulk at this and want to get it cheaper elsewhere (although this is far less likely than you would think, see my blogs on pricing www.rsaccountancy.co.uk/blog). So you could keep the fee at £1,000 and then pay the VAT over this way, in this case the VAT is £166.67 and your fee is £833.33. Which means that you have just dropped your price by 20%. If your profit margin is 20%, you are now making no money.

Another option is to split the difference between the customer and yourself. For example charging £900 + VAT which is £1,080.

My recommendation is that you don't absorb any of the VAT yourself since you are killing your profit. If your response is that your customers won't pay it then I would say get better customers. Change your business model where you are selling to VAT registered businesses who don't care about the VAT, or to rich individuals who can afford the VAT and who want to pay a VAT registered business because they are more trustworthy.

Also, if your customer base are VAT registered businesses you may want to consider becoming VAT registered before you have to (before you hit £82,000 sales) simply to look more credible and bigger than you are.

Four different types of ways to account for VAT

The first thing you have to do when you become VAT registered is start charging VAT on your sales invoices i.e. 20% on top of your normal fee/price.

So your invoice looks like this on a fee that you are charging to a customer of £1,000.

NET   £1,000

VAT   £200

GROSS   £1,200

The customer then pays you the £1,200.

You then have to make sure that you get VAT receipts for all your business expenditure so that you can claim the VAT back (only on option 1 and 2, see below).

However, if becoming VAT registered isn't complicated enough, you are then faced with 4 options of how to account for VAT.

Option 1 – VAT on invoices

You declare to HMRC all the VAT on your invoices in the quarter minus all the VAT on your purchase invoices and expenses.

This is the most common way of accounting for VAT.

Option 2 – VAT on cash

You declare to HMRC all the VAT on your sales receipts in the quarter minus all the VAT on your purchase invoices and expenses in the quarter.

The advantage of this is that you are only ever paying VAT over to HMRC that you have received from your customer. In option 1, you could pay VAT over to HMRC on an invoice that hasn't been paid yet.

The disadvantage of this is that it makes the bookkeeping more complicated.

Option 3 – VAT on invoices using the flat rate scheme

The flat rate scheme is for businesses of less than £150,000 turnover but since 1 April 2017, it is only worth going on it if you spend more than 2% of your sales on goods (goods means products, materials, stock and NOT services, utilities, sub-contractors, travel and subsistence).

Rather than option 1, you are assigned by HMRC a specific flat rate %. So for example 12%. The % is based on your type of business, you can find the current list here:

https://www.gov.uk/vat-flat-rate-scheme/vat-flat-rates

You then add up all your sales invoices and INCLUDE the VAT – i.e. you add up the GROSS amount of your invoices (the NET + the VAT = the GROSS) and then you multiply this amount by the flat rate %.

Sounds like a no brainer since your flat rate % will be lower than 20%. However, you COMPLETELY IGNORE the VAT on your expenditure.

(I say COMPLETELY IGNORE, there is a special rule that means you can still claim the VAT on 'capital costs' over £2,000 even on the flat rate scheme)

Option 4 – VAT on invoices cash the flat rate scheme

This is the same principle as option 3, it just means you add up the sales receipts (which will include the VAT) and apply the flat rate %.

The flat rate scheme was introduced by HMRC to make it easier for smaller businesses to account for VAT, it was not meant to save you VAT.

However, for certain businesses you will save VAT and the difference between option 1 and 2 and option 3 and 4 could be significant.

Generally speaking, if you don't have a huge amount of VATable expenditure then the flat rate scheme could save you VAT especially if your flat rate % for your industry is lower i.e. around the 12% mark. Another incentive for you to use the flat rate scheme is that you get a 1% discount on the industry flat rate in the first year AND accountants tend to charge less for flat rate VAT returns since they are much more straightforward.

I regularly calculate the difference between going on the flat rate scheme or using the more traditional method of option 1 and 2. If you would like me to do this for you, email me at russell@rsaccountancy.co.uk . The difference could be an annual VAT saving of up to £3,000 per year.

VAT MOSS

VAT MOSS is a piece of tax legislation that was introduced on 1 January 2015. It affects businesses that sell digital products to consumers in the EU (i.e. not business to business).

The complicated part is that you have to charge the customer the VAT rate applicable in the customer's EU country (i.e. not the UK rate 20%).

There are two additional burdens of this for businesses. Firstly, it is likely that digital products will be sold online and therefore all websites need to be coded to have the ability to change the VAT rate depending on the customer's country of origin. Secondly, as well as doing normal VAT returns, businesses have to do the VAT MOSS return as well every quarter.

The worst part though is that businesses who are not even VAT registered have to register for VAT MOSS.   This has caused some real problems and in some cases has meant the closure of businesses. There is a website set up to help with VAT MOSS called www.vateuaction.co.uk which is very useful.

If you would like more help on whether you have to comply with VAT MOSS email me at russell@rsaccountancy.co.uk.

CIS – Construction Industry Scheme

If your business falls into the construction industry scheme (for example, builders, electricians, decorators) then you have to comply with the construction industry scheme rules.

There are two main parts to this. Firstly, if you pay any subcontractors (not employees), you have to deduct 20% tax from them at source and pay this over to HMRC.

Secondly, your customers will do the same to you, so you will receive 20% less from your customers.

The CIS returns have to be completed monthly for deducting your subcontractors 20% and have to be submitted by the 19th of the month (the fines are £100 for non-compliance). The CIS that is taken from you by your customer is set off against your monthly payroll submissions.

If you end up with more CIS taken from you than you have paid out, you can claim the difference back from HMRC, although they are notoriously slow at paying.

CIS can be very onerous for businesses and adds a new complication to the bookkeeping. You can attempt to escape the CIS rules by applying for CIS Gross status. If you are successful you are able to not deduct 20% from your subcontractors and crucially not be deducted from your customers.

Chapter 7 – HMRC and Companies House deadlines

We live in a world of deadlines. When you become a business you are given lots more statutory deadlines and the worst thing is, most of them carry fines if you don't complete paperwork on time. This chapter is to make you aware of all the deadlines that you are subject to. It is true that your accountant should be on top of these and be able to communicate to you when tasks have to be done. However, I think it is useful if you know these as well and I would recommend putting all of these in your diary/online calendar.

If you are self-employed, you can ignore the Companies House deadlines.

Companies House deadlines (for limited companies)

Year-end accounts – 9 months after your year end

If you are a limited company you have to produce year end accounts. These are in a statutory format that only accountants will know how to produce (whilst it is possible for a self-employed individual to complete his own tax return, it is not possible for a business owner to do limited company accounts themselves, unless they are an accountant!).

The accounts are produced in two formats, an abbreviated set for Companies House and a full set (about 14 pages) for the Corporation Tax office.

The abbreviated set just contains a covering page, a balance sheet and one page of notes to the balance sheet.

The most important thing to know about these accounts are that they are publicly accessible. However, they don't really tell you much. Since there is no profit and loss account, a reader of the accounts (and they would have to be someone who understands how to read a balance sheet) would be able to see what the net assets number was on the balance sheet (see chapter 1) and how much cash was in the company but that's pretty much about it.

They would not know how much profit you were making, what your profit margins were or whether you had any sales growth year to year.

These year-end accounts have to be submitted to Companies House by nine months after your year end.

If it is your first year, your year end is the date that is the next month end after your incorporation date. So if you incorporated on 8 June 2015, your year end is 30 June 2016. Strangely, your first set of accounts would be due by 8 March 2016 and not 31 March 2016, although after the first year the deadline would always be 31 March 2016.

The fines for non-submission of Companies House accounts are steep. They are:

Up to 1 month overdue - £150

From 1 month to 3 months overdue - £375

Over 3 months overdue - £750

Over 6 months overdue - £1,500

If this isn't bad enough, the fines are doubled if you submit the accounts late two years in a row.

Unlike some HMRC fines, Companies House are notoriously hard to appeal against – the current success rate is 3.7%.

Confirmation statement – 14 days after your incorporation anniversary

Your annual return is a much simpler document than the year end accounts. It is essentially a confirmation that your company name, registered office, director and shareholder's details are the same. It doesn't take very long to do and can be completed online. It costs £13 to complete.

It has to be completed annually. Just before the anniversary date of your original incorporation date, you get issued with a letter requesting you to complete the annual return within 14 days of the incorporation anniversary date.

The request letter that Companies House send is bizarrely over the top, threatening you with a £5,000 fine and dire consequences if you don't complete the annual return. I guess someone at Companies House must have had a bad day when they drafted the letter because it truly is very scary looking. However, I have personally never known anybody fined £5,000 for late submission of an annual return. In contrast, the letter to complete the year end accounts is much more serene and I have rarely known anybody NOT to have to pay a fine if they submit the year end accounts late.

HMRC deadlines

For Limited companies

Year-end accounts and corporation tax return – 12 months after your year end (corporation tax payment due 9 months and 1 day after your year-end)

The first strange thing to notice is that the corporation tax return and year end accounts are due 12 months after the year end, whilst the corporation tax is actually due 9 months and 1 day after your year end. It is slightly bizarre, but in reality, your year-end accounts for Companies House AND HMRC will be completed within 9 months so you know what corporation tax to pay.

It is well worth putting the corporation tax due date in your calendar and ensure you build it into your cash flow since it could be a large sum that if not planned, could kill your cash flow.

Whilst you do have 9 months after the year end to complete the accounts and corporation tax return it is far better to complete this much earlier, my recommendation is within 3 months.

There are two reasons for this, firstly, so you know how you have performed – sales, profit and cash and secondly, so you know what the corporation tax amount is way in advance of having to pay it. If it is a large sum it is far better to know 6 months in advance than 6 days in advance.

The fine for non-submission of a corporation tax return is £100 (so not as large as the Companies House fines).

For both limited companies and self-employed individuals

Personal tax return for the year ended 5 April, due the following 31 January

Both self-employed individuals and directors of a limited company need to complete a personal tax return.

For the self-employed individual this will have on the numbers from the self-employed accounts plus any other income that there might be e.g. employment income, property income etc.

For the director of a limited company, the personal tax return will show dividends taken from the company, plus a minimum director salary in the employment section (see next chapter on tax). If the director also earns other income such as property income or employment income it will have this on as well.

For the self-employed individual, their accounts year end is 5 April and their personal tax return is 5 April. It is a little more complicated for the limited company directors. Whilst their personal tax return year end is 5 April (everybody's is), their company year-end will be the month after whenever they set the company up **(see Chapter above)**. This is a bit confusing for new limited companies to get their head round, they ultimately have two year ends. The way to look at it is that one year end is for the company and one year end is for the director's earnings – they are not the same thing.

Some businesses make their company year-end 31 March just to tie it up with the 5 April. Whilst I think it is useful to have 31 March as a year end, I don't think it is essential and wouldn't recommend changing your company year-end for this purpose (if you do want to change a company year-end it is relatively straightforward to do).

If you are wondering why the personal year end is 5 April and not something more sensible like a month end – 31 March or even 31 December, then have a look at my blog post on the subject where I tell you the whole historical story of why it is 5 April and the band of accountants who seek to change it to 31 March (the story is too long to record here but if you are interested, check out my blog on www.rsaccountancy.co.uk/daily-blog).

The deadline for all personal tax returns (for both self-employed individuals and directors of limited companies) is 31 January. This is actually a full 10 months after the year end and is one of the longest deadlines in Europe (in the US they have only 3 and half months). A few years ago, this did look like it would be changed but the accountancy profession successfully lobbied against it.

If you submit the tax return late, you are given a £100 fine. In recent years, HMRC (like Companies House) have ramped up the fines on late submission. They are now as follows:

If it is 1 day late - you get hit with a fine of £100

It is then £10 for each day over 31 January 2015, up to 30 April 2015 (90 days) at which point, the extra fine will be £900. Add on the original £100 and it is £1,000.

If you still haven't submitted it by 31 July 2015, the fine will be an additional £300 or 5% of the tax, whichever is the highest. The fine now totals £1,300.

If you still haven't submitted it by 31 January 2015, the fine goes up by another £300 (or 5% of the tax) which means that your total fine is £1,600.

These are only fines relating to not submitting a tax return.

There are also the fines and interest on not paying the income tax.

Please also note, if you do a paper tax return, these have to be in by 31 October.

Payroll

Payroll for employees or yourself has to be submitted monthly by the end of the month. The PAYE tax deadline is 19th of the following month.

Whilst you may not have employees, it still may be tax efficient to put yourself through the payroll as a minimum salary (see Chapter 7 on paying yourself).

There is more information on payroll in Chapter 8.

The payroll deadlines also apply to CIS.

P11Ds

P11D forms are needed if your company has given you something that has not gone through the payroll. The technical word is a 'benefit-in-kind'.

Common examples of this are company cars or private medical insurance.

You declare these 'benefit-in-kinds' on the P11D form up to the personal tax year end and these have to be submitted to HMRC by 6 July.

VAT returns

VAT returns are usually quarterly (although you can opt to do them annually). The quarter ends depend on when you first become VAT registered. Your first VAT return can be slightly random e.g. it could be one month or five months! After the first VAT return it will be every three months.

It is well worth syncing up your quarterly VAT return quarter ends with your limited company year- end since this makes the accounts much easier. The original VAT return quarters set by HMRC can be changed.

The deadline is one month and 7 days after the quarter end i.e. if your quarter end is 31 March, then your VAT return has to be submitted by 7 May. Payment also has to be made by this date, although if you set up a direct debit with HMRC you are able to get a few more days credit.

Most people in business are a bit intimidated by the VAT department as they have heard horror stories of severe fines and crackdowns.

Unfortunately these stories are often true as the VAT return penalties are even worse than the Companies House and Personal tax return penalties.

HMRC can charge you for late filing and late payment of VAT amounts. They apply percentages of the outstanding amount and these escalate if you are late more than once.

The first thing to do if you know you are struggling to pay your VAT bill is to speak to your accountant as there are always options about what to do (e.g. payment plans, changing the way you account for VAT).

Chapter 8 – Estimating and paying the tax

Introduction

There are a few major advantages of either being a self-employed individual or an owner of a limited company over being an employee.

Firstly, you do pay less tax. You get to charge expenses to your income that you would not have been able to as an employee and the overall tax rates are lower. Generally at the basic rate of tax – 19% for a limited company, 29% for a self-employed individual and 32% for an employee.

Secondly, you get to account for the tax yourself. When you are an employee, you receive your monthly payslip every month net of any tax taken off and the amount appears in your bank account (I bet you assumed that your employer calculated the tax correctly, let's hope they did!!!). Now, you are the person who deducts the tax, but you don't do this on a monthly basis. You will pay HMRC either once a year (limited company) or twice a year (self-employed individual).

The good news is that you get to keep money in your bank account that is due to HMRC for a long time which means you can earn interest, use it for working capital or just feel comfortable with a big bank balance. The bad news is that when HMRC come looking for their money, you'd better know what the amount is and have it ready for them.

The second most difficult thing about completing your cash flow forecast (after predicting when your customers are going to pay you) is managing to pay the large amounts of tax that will hit your cash flow like an asteroid. What this Chapter aims to do is help you predict your tax amount so that it doesn't come as a huge shock.

The first rule of predicting your tax

You do actually get plenty of time between when your financial year comes to a close and when the tax is due (10 months for self-employment, 9 months for limited company – if you don't think this is enough, it is actually very generous compared to other EU countries and the US).

This means that you want to be predicting it as early as possible ideally every month. But it also means that you can confirm the tax amounts if you get your accounts info to your accountant early. Then the accountant can complete your accounts and confirm what the tax amount actually is.

In my firm, we encourage our clients to get their information to us within 3 months of the financial year end. It is bad enough having a conversation with a client when the tax bill is surprisingly high six months before the tax due but it is much worse having the same conversation a few days before it has to be paid.

Don't let this happen to you, commit to following the rules below and start estimating your tax as you go along and then get your estimate confirmed by your accountant way before the tax deadline.

If you are a self-employed individual, there is no real need to read the limited company Chapter and vice versa.

Before we get into the detail, you must know this….

It is always better to make money and pay tax then to make less money and pay less tax. This is because for every £100 you make, no matter what tax rate you pay, you will always have more money in your pocket than if you hadn't made the £100 in the first place.

Also, the different tax rates only apply to the money earned over the tax rate. For example, the top rate of income tax is 45% for those who earn over £150,000. However, you only ever pay 45% tax on the amount of money you earn over £150,000, you don't pay tax at 45% on your first £150,000.

Tax for the self-employed individual

In my meetings with newly self-employed individuals, I always say to them that the best thing about being self-employed is that you don't need to pay the tax until 10 months after their financial year closes. However, the worst thing is that you usually have to pay one year and a half's worth of tax in one go!

It's true, HMRC don't always make it that easy for you to manage your finances. They give you a massive grace period and then hit you with a tax bill over the odds. This chapter will show you how to use this to your advantage.

When is my financial year?

Everybody who is a self-employed individual has a year end of 5 April. So it doesn't matter what date you started your self-employment, your first year end will be 5 April and then your next year end will be the following 5 April.

For example, let's say you started self-employment on 15 June 2016.

Year one – 15 June 2015 to 5 April 2017

Year two – 6 April 2017 to 5 April 2018

Year three – 6 April 2018 to 5 April 2019

And so on….

When do I pay the tax?

This question depends on how much tax you have to pay. If your annual tax bill is lower than £1,000 then you only pay your tax once a year – always on the following 31 January.

So in this example, it looks like this:

Start self-employment 15 June 2016

Year one – 15 June 2016 to 5 April 2017 - Tax deadline – 31 January 2018

Year two – 6 April 2017 to 5 April 2018 – Tax deadline – 31 January 2019

Year three – 6 April 2018 to 5 April 2019 – Tax deadline – 31 January 2020

And so on….

If you are wondering whether your tax bill will be over £1,000. You would have to earn PROFITS (not sales income) of approximately £17,500 to have a tax bill of £1,000 on your self-employment earnings.

76

If your tax bill is over £1,000 (i.e. on PROFITS, not sales income of approximately £17,500) then it is a different story.

Bear with me on this. This is one of the most complicated things about self-employed tax to get your head around.

If your tax bill is over £1,000 then HMRC will ask you to pay one year and half of tax i.e. you pay your tax on your year's profit but you also pay another 50%.

The immediate question is, how do HMRC know what your profits will be next year? The simple answer is 'they don't', they just assume you are going to earn the same (obviously never the case) so they just charge you 50% on your current profit.

So, for example...

Start self-employment 15 June 2016

Year one – 15 June 2016 to 5 April 2017 - Tax deadline – 31 January 2018 - Tax due on this year - £1,000. Tax charged by HMRC - £1,500.

This extra tax charged is for the next year and will go against next year's bill. You will then be expected to pay another 50% to next year's bill on 31 July. By the time it comes to the next 31 January, your entire bill should be paid off (if your tax bill is the same). Alas, this doesn't mean you have nothing to pay, HMRC ask you to pay another 50% for the next year.

So here is how it looks with two years when your tax bills are exactly the same.

Start self-employment 15 June 2016

Year one – 15 June 2016 to 5 April 2017 - Tax deadline – 31 January 2018 - Tax due on this year - £1,000. Tax charged by HMRC - £1,500 (The £500 going against the tax bill for 5 April 2018)

Year two – 6 April 2017 to 5 April 2018 – Tax deadline – 50% - £500 for 31 January 2018 and 50% - £500 for 31 July 2018

Year three – 6 April 2018 to 5 April 2019 – Tax deadline – 50% - £500 for 31 January 2019 and 50% - £500 for 31 July 2019

You can see here that what started as a very long grace period has now shrunk somewhat as in year two, you are effectively paying 50% of your tax bill by 31 January 2018, two months before your end of the financial year – 5 April 2018.

HMRC's term for this is 'payment on account'. However, businesses term this 'payment up front'. Technically, it isn't a payment up front since the tax is due on 31 January and this represents the first 50% of the financial year – 6 April to 5 October. So you still get four months grace period but I guarantee it won't feel like it.

There is an immediate problem with HMRC's assumption. It is highly likely that your tax bill next year will not be the same. Usually it is higher, meaning that you may be thinking that you have paid 50% of your tax bill but in reality you have paid much less of it.

The above example is okay from a theoretical sense but in truth, your tax bills will vary (and go up if your business is successful). Here is a more true-life example:

Start self-employment 15 June 2016

Tax year

Year one – 15 June 2016 to 5 April 2017 - Tax amount - £1,000 Tax deadline – 31 January 2018 - Tax due on this year - £1,000. Tax charged by HMRC - £1,500 (The £500 going against the tax bill for 5 April 2018)

Year two – 6 April 2017 to 5 April 2018 – Tax amount - £2,000 Tax deadline – 50% - £1000 for 31 January 2018 and 50% - £1,000 for 31 July 2018

Year three – 6 April 2018 to 5 April 2019 – Tax amount - £3,000 Tax deadline – 50% - £1,500 for 31 January 2019 and 50% - £1,500 for 31 July 2019

So, you can see that the tax goes up and up and the payments on account vary.

If you are sure that the financial year just passed has been uncharacteristically good, you can ask HMRC to reduce the payment on account on the basis that you will earn less next year. You have to be careful though, if you pay less on the payment on account and end up earning more, HMRC will charge you interest (although HMRC's interest is just 3.5% much less than other sources of finance).

If this chapter has left you baffled and confused feel free to email me at russell@rsaccountancy.co.uk. It does take self-employed businesses a while to get their heads round this.

What tax do I actually pay?

The first rule to understand is that your tax return will include all income. This is because all income sits on top of each other. For example:

Employed income - £10,000

Self-employed income - £10,000

Property income - £10,000 income

Dividends income - £10,000 income

Total income - £40,000 income

There is actually a certain order to how the income sits on top of each other. The dividends always sit on top, the property next, then the self-employed income, then the employed income.

For most newly self-employed individuals, there may be employment income from a previous job or ongoing employment income (it is completely fine to be self-employed and employed at the same time).

One quick thing to understand is that there are three different types of tax for the self-employed – Income Tax, National Insurance Class 2 and National Insurance Class 4.

Two of these are TAXES! Income tax (obviously) and National Insurance Class 4 (not so obvious). When you think about what national insurance contributions actually are i.e. contributions to your state pension, then it is only Class 2 that does this. Class 4 doesn't do anything for you at all, it is purely a tax.

So when I tell clients that they will pay 29% of tax as a self-employed individual, they often say "but isn't the income tax rate 20%". Yes it is but you have to pay Class 4 at 9% which is a tax, the same as income tax, even though the name is different!

In the examples below I am using the word tax to describe both tax and National Insurance Class 4.

Here is how the tax rates work for the self-employed:

For the year 2019-20 income up to £8,632 is completely tax free.

Income between £8,632 and £12,500 is 9% (just Class 4, nothing for income tax)

Income between £12,500 and £50,000 is 29% (20% income tax, 9% National Insurance Class 4)

Income after £50,000 is 42% (40% income tax, 2% National Insurance Class 4)

So here's an example:

Self-employment profit of £30,000.

First £8,632 – 0%

Second £3,868 – 9% = £348.12

Next £17,500 – 29% = £5075.00

Total £30,000, Tax is £5,423.12

Here's another example:

Self-employment profit of £60,000

First £8,632 – 0%

Second £3,868 – 9% = £348.12

Next £37,500 – 29% = £10,875

Next £10,000 – 42% = £4,200

Total £60,000, Tax is £15,423.12

You will also have to pay Class 2 NI which is £156 per year.

If this is becoming confusing, then try this quick solution….

If you are a self-employed individual and you earn less than £50,000 then if you put aside:

20% of all your sales invoices, you should have enough money to pay the tax at the end of the year. It is likely, you would end up with a bit of a bonus for yourself as well.

In all likelihood, you could push it to 18% but 20% is more of a safe bet.

Remember, this is 20% of your sales invoices, not 20% of your profits. You are taxed on your profits but if I give you a rule of thumb about your profits then you would have to calculate your profits every time you want to estimate the tax and this isn't always practicable.

Don't forget the payments on account

If you follow the 20% rule above (or 18% if you want to be more risky), you really can't go wrong, you will always have enough money for the tax whenever the taxman wants it, be it the big one year and half tax bombshell or the more sedate six monthly tax bills.

Once you get over the big tax bombshell, life will become slightly easier, paying the tax every 6 months.

You don't have to follow my 20% rule

One of the advantages of being self-employed is that you don't actually need to save for your tax. You can do whatever you like with the money, it really doesn't matter. The only thing that matters is that you pay the tax on time. This is why my 20% rule works and means that you won't ever be scratching your head or stressed out if you haven't got enough to pay the tax.

Tax for the limited company

Tax for the limited company is much more straightforward than being self-employed as the tax bands are easier to understand and there are no payments on account.

There is only one tax you pay as a company and that is corporation tax. As a shareholder, you can potentially pay tax on your dividends (drawings from the company), I will cover this in the next Chapter.

Corporation tax is 19% of your profits.

Here's how this works:

Sales	£50,000
Costs	£10,000
Profit	£40,000
Corporation tax – 19%	£7,600
Profit after tax	£32,400

As you can see, it is a straight 19% of your profits. It is crucial to make sure you have recorded all your costs since if you don't you will artificially increase your profits and therefore increase your tax.

The profit after tax of £32,400 is for the shareholder. There is no tax on this until you begin to draw it out of the company – see next Chapter....

Chapter 9 – How to pay yourself

Introduction

In the last Chapter we talked about estimating and paying the tax. The next complication of running your own tax affairs is how much to pay yourself. There are three elements to this. Firstly, what is the most tax efficient way to pay yourself – both how to do it and how much? Secondly, how do you know you are not paying yourself too much i.e. have you left enough for the taxman, and thirdly, how do I know I am not taking too much from the business generally i.e. leaving enough cash in to run the business.

Paying yourself as a self-employed individual

The beauty of being a self-employed individual (sole trader) is that it is very easy to pay yourself. How do you pay yourself? You just pay yourself.

Transfer money from your business account into your personal account. If you don't have a business account (remember you don't need to have one), just spend the money. Nobody cares what you do with the money that you earn from your customers except for the fateful day, be it 31 January or 31 July, when the taxman comes knocking at your door asking for his tax. So you'd better have the money put aside (see last Chapter) or be able to produce the money on the required date.

The big downside of being self-employed is that you are taxed on profits no matter what you do. It is simply, your income less your expenses equals your profit. You are then automatically taxed on your profits and there's not too much you can do it about it.

However, paying yourself is easy from a self-employed point of view.

Paying yourself as a limited company

Paying yourself from a limited company is more complicated than self-employment for two reasons.

Firstly, you have to pay yourself in two different ways and secondly, you have to have paperwork in place to make it legitimate.

There is a single most tax efficient way to pay yourself as a limited company (assuming you don't have any other income). This has been similar advice for the last 6-7 years.

First, pay yourself a salary

Pay yourself a salary of £8,632 and dividends of £41,368 if you are a one person company or a salary of £12,500 and dividends of £37,500 if you are a two person company.

Here's how this works for the one person company.

Sales	£60,000
Expenses	-£10,000
Profit	£50,000
Corporation tax 19%	-£9,500
Profit after tax	£40,500

You pay corporation tax on your profits – a straight 19%. The best way of saving corporation tax is to make sure you have all your costs included.

What is left after corporation tax is yours to take (as long as the cash is in the business i.e. all your customers have paid you).

However, you can do something clever before you take the £40,500. You can put through a salary of £8,632. The reason why it is £8,632 is that this means that you pay no income tax (since it is the personal allowance – the amount that everybody receives tax free) and no national insurance.

The best bit is that you get 19% corporation tax deduction on it. Which means you pay yourself £8,632 income tax free and then get a corporation tax saving of £1,640.08.

Here's how this works....

Sales   £60,000

Expenses   -£10,000

Salary   -£8,632

Profit   £41,368

Corporation tax -£7,860 (a saving of £1,640 from the above example)

Profit after tax   £33,508

Be warned, if you are using up your £8,632 personal allowance through other income e.g. employment, property or investment income, you do not then want to pay yourself more salary since whilst it will still get a corporation tax saving of 19% you will pay income tax and national insurance on the salary of 32%. Not good!

It is more tax efficient to pay a salary of £8,632 than £12,500 (the tax free personal allowance) because you pay more national insurance on the amount between £8,632 and £12,500 than the corporation tax saving on the increased salary.

HOWEVER, if you are a two person company you can claim the 'employment allowance' through the payroll which wipes out part of the national insurance making it more tax efficient to pay £12,500.

For a detailed calculation of this, email me at russell@rsaccountancy.co.uk.

Secondly, pay yourself dividends up to £50,000 income (the higher rate of tax)

So if you pay £8,632 salary, pay dividends to £41,368. If you pay £12,500 salary, pay £37,500 dividends.

Here's how this works:

Sales	£70,000
Expenses	-£10,000
Salary	-£8,632
Profit	£51,368
Corporation tax	-£9,760
Profit after tax	£41,608
Dividends	-£41,368
Profit left	£240

The new dividend tax sadly arrived on 6 April 2016. Before this tax, you could take dividends out of a limited company up to the basic rate (up to £39,206) income-tax free and pay 25% tax in the higher rate.

Now you only get £2,000 of dividends income-tax free, the rest is taxed at 7.5% and then when you go past £41,368 dividends you pay a whopping 32.5% tax on the amounts above.

Even worse, you have already suffered 19% of corporation tax before you take out the dividends.

Here's the tax on the 2 salary/dividend options...

Salary	£8,632	£12,500
Dividends	£41,368	£37,500
Tax free amount	-£2,000	-£2,000
Dividends covered in personal allowance	-£3,868	-
Dividends to be taxed	£35,500	£35,500
Tax @ 7.5%	£2,662.50	£2,662.50

Here is the big catch on the new dividend tax:

Small limited companies have enjoyed paying no income tax for many years (as long as they kept their dividends below the higher rate of tax).

This is now going to change.

There will definitely be some amount of income tax charge.

Here's the catch.

If your income tax bill is over £1,000, then HMRC will want you to pay 50% for next year in the same payment (same rules as self employment)

So following the £2,662.50 tax bill above, this would turn into:

Income tax bill	- £2,662.50
50% payment on account	- £1,331.25
Total income tax bill	- £3,993.75

The good news is that in the year ended 5 April 2020, you won't need to pay this until 31 January 2021.

But when you do need to pay it, it could be a hefty amount with the 50% payment on account.

AND HERE'S THE REAL CATCH……

If you don't have the money saved personally to pay HMRC and you have to take more dividends from your limited company to pay the tax, you will therefore be taxed again on the dividends you have taken to pay tax!!!

It is like a tax cycle of death.

You take salary and dividends up to £50,000 to avoid the 32.5% higher rate of tax but forget to put aside the money to pay the income tax. You then take out more dividends, therefore tipping you into the 32.5% tax band – ouch!

I've got a very tasty spreadsheet that I've used with clients to predict what their tax bill will be on 31 January 2021 and to avoid this tax cycle of death. If you'd like this spreadsheet email me at russell@rsaccountancy.co.uk

A couple more things on dividends to keep your eyes on

Firstly, unlike self-employment individuals, you can't just take out what you want. It is illegal to take out dividends higher than your profits after tax which means that you need to keep the taxman's money in the company. (There are legal ways around this though see next chapter on director loan accounts).

Also, whilst your profit and loss account may say that you have profits so feel free to take them out, your bank account may say a different thing. If your bank account hasn't got any cash in it, you won't be able to take the dividend.

Secondly, you need to keep up to date dividend documentation. This involves a record of a board meeting of the directors where they vote for a dividend and issue a dividend voucher to the shareholder. If you would like a template of this feel free to email me at russell@rsaccountancy.co.uk

There's another catch and this is where it gets strange. You can keep all of your business documentation digitally, you don't need the paper copy EXCEPT dividend documentation. This must be kept in paper form. I have no idea why, that's just the way it is!

Often, in the rush to get the dividends out of the bank account, businesses then forget to do the paperwork but it must be kept. If HMRC do investigate you, this is one of the first things that they look for.

You are allowed to pay yourself monthly dividends but do keep the paperwork!

Director loan accounts

A Director loan account is the rolling balance of whether the director is owed any money FROM the company or whether they owe anything TO the company.

A common example is where the director has incurred company expenses on a personal debit card and needs to claim back this money from the company. In this case the company owes the director.

This is going to happen quite a bit, especially in the early days, but you really want to try your hardest to keep all company expenses in the company bank account. It just saves time and hassle.

However, if a director takes too much out of the company and so it cannot be called dividends (since you can't take out more dividends than there is profit) it therefore must be a director loan i.e. the company has lent money to the director. You may think that this would be a useful way of taking more than the £41,368 dividends tax-free and you would be right to a point.

The trouble is, if you have an overdrawn director loan account at the year end (i.e. the director owes the company) you have 9 months to pay it back. You can either physically pay it back in cash or you declare a dividend on paper but don't actually pay yourself.

If you do not pay back the loan within 9 months, you will be hit with a 32.5% tax charge. Which is coincidentally, the same % as the income tax charge on dividends of over £41,368. There is one difference this is a tax charge on the loan. If you pay the loan back you will get the tax back.

Generally though, you want to avoid this at all costs.

Free dividend report

I wrote a free dividend report on the new dividend tax and how to avoid it. If you would like a free report on these changes, email me at russell@rsaccountancy.co.uk

Chapter 10 – Employing people

Introduction

Once you've started your business and began to grow it, you'll come to the awful realisation that you can't do everything yourself – you need help.

Personally, I found the leap between employment and self-employment to be very easy (even though I did it in a very high risk way i.e. zero clients from day one). I became self-employed because I wanted to be my own boss, to get up when I wanted and not to have to work with other team members.

However, then the business got bigger and I needed help. I procrastinated for a long time before I hired my first person and I certainly found the leap between self-employment to manager to be a tricky one. Once I hired my first person, I didn't stop and then accidentally lost all my new found freedom and flexibility that I had as a self-employed individual (but hey, working at home on my own did get lonely and it is much more fun running a business with lots of fun people).

If you are at the point where you are thinking of getting help you have a choice – do you employ or get a freelancer?

To employ or get a freelancer?

Get a freelancer – advantages

You'll probably find them quicker because they will be out looking for work and more visible.

You can use them for a few hours a week or a more concentrated period.

You can drop them at a moment's notice.

You don't pay Employer tax i.e. no Employer National Insurance.

You don't have the burden of HR law that comes with employment.

Useful to dip your toe in employment without actually employing anybody officially, especially when you are starting your business

No appraisals!

Get a freelancer - disadvantages

They will cost more, have an hourly rate (and almost certainly cost more than an employee even with Employers National Insurance.

It is difficult to build a company vision with freelancers.

You may not be able to keep them – they could get too busy with other projects and you have no 'ownership' of them.

Get an employee - advantages

You have the chance of hiring someone who can have a huge impact on your company.

Their commitment will be (should be!) more than a freelancer, not just to the delivery of the work but to other aspects of the business as well.

Harder for them to leave or be poached by a competitor.

Likely to be cheaper than a freelancer (even with holiday and sick pay)

You can plan your business around them

Get an employee – disadvantages

You have to officially become an 'employer'.

You have to manage payroll or pay someone to do it.

You have to pay the taxman some more tax (PAYE/NI) as well as net pay to the employee – more complication and timing problems for your cash flow.

If you've got nothing for them to do, you still have to pay them.

If they don't work out, it is more difficult to let them go than a freelancer.

If they don't work, they are more likely to mess with your brain and emotions than a freelancer will have the power to do!

You have to have an understanding of HR law so that you know what you are responsible for.

You need Employers Public Liability Insurance.

You have to pay them holidays.

Worse than that, you have to pay them sick (if they are sick!).

You'll need to appraisals!

Personally, I have always loved employing people but then I am more of a EON guy (Everything or Nothing) but it may not work for you especially if you are just starting.

So let's see what you have to do if you do get someone on a board...

What do you need to do for a freelancer?

Hardly anything actually. You agree an hourly or day rate and they invoice you. You then pay them. That's it.

What do you need to do for an employee payroll?

Lots. You'll need an employment contract first of all (an HR company or lawyer can do this for you or you could get a generic one of the web). This contract will confirm pay and number of holidays. If you have a part-time employee, make sure you pro-rata the salary.

When they commence employment, you'll need to first set yourself up as an Employer and set them up as an employee.

You then pay them monthly with a payslip, but you don't pay them like you would a freelancer.

You pay them a monthly apportionment of their annual salary less the PAYE/NI.

This is where it gets tricky.

Say, you hire someone at salary of £24,000.

They start on July 1.

At the end of the month you pay them 1/12 of their salary which is £2,000.

Here is what it will say on the payslip.

Gross salary £2,000

Less PAYE (20% after the first £1,041.67 which is £12,500 annually) - £191.67

Less National Insurance (12% after the first £664 per month) - £160.32

Total deductions - £351.99

Net pay £1,648.01

You would pay the employee on the last day of the month but you always pay the net pay to the employee.

You then have to pay the following to HMRC by the 22nd of the following month:

PAYE taken from employee - £191.67

National Insurance taken from employee - £160.32

AND

Employers national insurance
(13.8% of the amount over £664 per month, in this case £1,336 x 13.8%) - £184.37

Total to pay £536.36

So in total you are paying your employee £1,648.01 and the taxman £536.36. Your total cost for employment is £2,184.37 (£2,000 + £184.37)

Notice, this is more than the £2,000 per month you first thought. This is because of the Employers National Insurance (13.8% over £664 per month).

My rule of thumb is, think of the salary and add on 10%, this is the true cost of an employee (in this case it is add on 9%).

You can ask an accountant or a payroll bureau to run the payroll for you or you can do it yourself on HMRC software.

I personally recommend getting someone to do it since even if you master the basic deductions above, it can get a load more complicated when you are faced with:

Maternity pay

Sick pay

Holiday pay

Student loan repayments

It is also worth getting an HR advisor on board to give ongoing HR and legal advice.

Chapter 11 – Property

A great businessman, Brad Sugars from actionCOACH, once said in a book that the correct order to create wealth is to:

Build a business

Invest in a property portfolio with the returns from the business

Invest in stocks and shares

Unfortunately, many people start dabbling in property before they have actually grown a successful business or the cash flow to really get good deals on property. In any case, you may want to invest in a buy-to-let or actually build a property trading or property investment business. Or maybe you simply want to get a mortgage.

There is a few crucial things you need to know before embarking on this quest.

The BIG problem with getting a mortgage.

Pre 2008, getting a mortgage was one of the easiest things in the world.

Since the financial crash of 2008, it has been increasingly difficult for anybody to get a mortgage but if you are self-employed, a freelancer or a contractor it can be even harder.

If you are employed, you can pretty much produce 3 months payslips and most mortgage providers will give you a mortgage providing you earn enough.

The trouble with being self-employed, freelance or a contractor is that you are viewed as a higher risk since (in their eyes) you don't have a 'real job' or you don't have steady employment.

You can produce your tax return or your accounts but they will often need an accountant to verify the numbers and in some cases, predict the future profitability of your self-employment.

There is also something very important for you to know…..

Good accountants will always be trying to save you tax. They will do this by reducing your profits by making sure you have all the legitimate costs in the business. The trouble is that this may go against your desire to get the property of your dreams since you may need your income to be higher.

Also, mortgage companies will often look at your personal tax return and not your limited company accounts. Which means it becomes less about what you actually earn (how much profit you have made in the year) and more about what you have taken out of the company. So you sort of get penalised for leaving money in your company.

There's two ways around these problems….

Firstly, tell your accountant when you are just beginning to think about moving and secondly, get a decent mortgage broker who can communicate with the mortgage provider and will be able to bring in the limited company accounts numbers as well as the tax return.

To buy a property you need CASH

OK, that sounds really obvious. Let me explain what I mean.

Pre 2008, I had a conversation with someone who wanted advice on having a property portfolio with 'no money down'. This was jargon for not putting a deposit down. Which basically meant that this individual was going to end up with 20 properties without actually putting any cash in. Sounds crazy? That's because it was.

Post 2008, nobody is really asking for advice like this. However, there are some people that think buying property is easy i.e. get your first property, watch it grow in value then leverage the debt to buy your second. This works well, if the market is always growing, less well when it isn't (which contrary to the pre 2008 belief, does actually happen).

So you need cash for your first deposit (since 2008, these deposit percentages have increased as lenders have become more cautious) and you need cash to manage the downside risk of the property values decreasing and work that may be needed on your property (not to mention dodgy tenants not paying rent!).

Chapter 12 – Insurance

Do I need to be insured as a contractor/freelancer?

The quick answer is YES.

You will need the following:

Public Liability insurance – to insure you against injury or death to third parties and damage to third party property as a result of your actions.

Professional Indemnity Insurance – to insure you against any claims made against you.

Employer Liability insurance – not needed if you are the only employee and own at least 50% of the shares.

Chapter 13 – Getting clients and customers

Introduction

One of the great fears of going self-employed is giving up a steady job. Paradoxically, after you have built up a portfolio of clients and customers you can end up in a much more secure position financially. This is because your employer can decide to get rid of you at any time and there is only 1 employer. If you are self-employed and have lots of clients and customers the chance of them all getting rid of you at the same time is highly improbable. Even if that happens you can find new customers quickly, often much quicker than finding a new job.

So, getting to this position should be your first goal. Once you have set everything up and got your head around everything that you've got to do to run a business, growing your business to a comfortable size should be your priority.

You may think that the best businesses are the ones with the best people, best product, best service, best business leaders. This is rarely the case. The best businesses are the ones with the best sales and marketing.

1 - Decide what sort of business you want

Before you get good at sales and marketing, decide what sort of business you want. Do you want to build an empire with lots of employees working for you whilst you don't do much work, or do you love the work you do and don't fancy managing a team? It's better to be honest about what you want now since otherwise the opportunities that you will have will dictate this for you. This will also inform your pricing. If you are a one person business that is GREAT at what you will do, then you will be able to charge higher prices.

2 - Decide who your best customers are

This is another thing that most businesses don't do. They don't decide which customers are the best for them. This is mainly because they start their business, acquire anybody as customers because they need the work then as the business builds they decide that they then can't afford to get rid of customers that they don't want.

The trick is to decide at the outset what service you are going to offer and what customers you are going to offer it to and DON'T DEVIATE from this even when you are tempted (and you will be).

3 - Find out where your customers hang out

Once you have identified who your best customers are, you then have to find out where these people are. Do they belong to associations? Are they on social media? Are they local or across the UK? Are they are a certain age?

Whatever you do, don't go down the road of saying that your customers could be ANYONE! Anyone means NO ONE. Be specific.

4 - In the beginning do marketing that doesn't cost anything

When you start a business, the last thing you want to do is to spend lots of money on expensive marketing. You really don't need to if you do the following exercise.

Grab a piece of paper, put yourself in the middle (draw a picture of yourself if you must). Then write down 10 people around you that you know who may know the sort of customers that you are after (notice, I didn't say 10 people that you can sell to!). Then, invite the 10 people for a coffee (individually), tell them what you are up to and ask them for their help in finding your ideal customers. You will be amazed at how helpful people will be.

5 - The key to sales – follow up

When you are meeting a prospective client, ALWAYS follow up with them. Follow up with them until they have said yes, no, or they need more time. Never lose control of the process and always do what you say you will do. But most importantly FOLLOW UP.

6 - Ask for referrals from everyone you do work for

If you have done a good job for someone, they will be inclined to refer you. However, they won't refer you if you don't' ask (or highly unlikely to).

Quick tip, don't ask 'do you know anybody who may benefit from my service?', ask 'who do you know who would benefit from my service?'. The first line won't produce referrals, the second line will.

There is a ton of information out there on sales and marketing, some of it okay, some of it good and some of it great. However, it starts with your commitment to get good at it. It may not be natural to you but if you want to grow a business, there will be some elements of sales and marketing that you will need.

Chapter 14 – Russell's top 10 tips to business success

Here are 10 very random tips that I have picked up over 10 years of being a business. I had a nice well-paid secure job but got bored and launched into self-employment (without any clients unfortunately). After acquiring clients and getting too busy, I realised that I needed team (and needed to get good at managing them). After 10 years of growing my business here are the top 10 things that I have found, hope you like them!

1 - Don't read the papers or listen to the news

Being self-employed is tough. One of the things you will need in abundance is POSITIVITY. If you read the papers or listen to the news, you would have noticed that any positive stories are outnumber 10 to 1 to negative stories.

Around the world every day, millions of beautiful, life affirming, amazing things happen. None of this is reported. What is reported is the worst stuff. Do you really need to know this 'news'? I'd suggest not. It's your call, of course. But you will be amazed at the difference of not having the world's news in your head in the morning.

I've grown my business through 'the worst financial crash since the 1930s' (apparently), a 'double-dip recession'. Do you think I grew my business because I listened to the loud voices of the media shouting about how everything was disastrous? Nope, the opposite! I decided to live without them.

2 - Get around positive people

In tip no. 1, I'm asking you to get rid of newspapers and the news. I'll go further....get rid of negative people in your life.

Again, to emphasise, growing a business is HARD. You need to stack the dice in your favour as much as possible. You need positive, supportive people around you 100% of the time.

If you keep your negative friends around you, they will hold you back. Once you start showing signs of success – will they be happy for you? Not in the slightest. Your success will show up what they are doing wrong in their own life and they won't like it (I think it's called 'tall poppy' syndrome and it's not nice).

Now, some of these negative people may be family members and I admit this is trickier. However, your negative family members may have double the power over you than your friends (since you are more likely to listen to their negativity). Take them in small doses but at the very least, identify the impact they are having over you.

If these first two tips seem a bit drastic, then just have a look around you and assess the people you are with. If your ambition for your business starts to wane, start hanging around with positive can-do people, you will notice the difference immediately.

3 - Who customers buy from is more important than what

The chances are, there are thousands of people who do the same thing you do. Some will be better, some will be worst but you are unlikely to be the best in the universe. However, there is nobody like you and if people like you and want to do business with YOU, then nobody can take away that USP.

4 - Get good at sales and marketing

Every business is a sales and marketing business. Even if you may not want to take over the world, there will be elements of sales and marketing that you need to learn.

If you get good at this, you will beat your competitors. Since they will just be concerned with 'doing the work'. No time to do sales and marketing learning as well as your day job? Well, your day job pays your wages whereas your evening learning will build your fortune.

5 - Don't undervalue yourself – get your prices right

It is such a temptation to lower your prices once you start your business because you just want the work. Don't do it! It will come back to bite you. Charge what you are worth and know what you are worth.

6 - Pay attention to attitudes to money

If you have any hang-ups on money (and most people do!), you want to get rid of those as soon as you can. There isn't space here to go into detail but negative attitudes towards money will hold you and your business growth back.

I've lost count of people I know in business who have said that they aren't doing it for the money or aren't that bothered about the money. Well, all I can say is, don't moan when you are working very hard and the money doesn't show up. Working hard does not equal wealthy person (despite what they teach in school).

7 - Keep on top of your costs but understand that revenue increases your profits

You need to be aware of your overheads and of the margins you are making on your team but it is revenue that will drive your business. There is a limit to how much you can decrease your expenditure but there is no limit to how you can increase your revenue.

8 - Read, listen and learn as much about business as you can

From the age of 5, I trained 19 years to become a qualified chartered accountant. 6 years at primary school, GCSES 5 years later, 'A' levels 2 years later, a degree (in Theology, no less) 3 years later and then another 3 years working as a trainee accountant and studying and taking exams in the evening. At 24, I become a qualified chartered accountant.

Guess how long I trained to be a business owner. Er, I didn't. I just set up a business.

I wish I was learning business since I was 5.

9 - Network wherever you go

I went to a café in Manchester the other day and had a hazelnut chocolate milkshake. They actually put a blended Toblerone in it. It tasted lovely, though the sugar rush was immense.

I walked out of the café with a prospect (the café owner). Network wherever you go. Your family, your friends, sports, music, politics, church.

All of your spheres – be on the lookout for opportunities. Not like some sales crazed wolf but as someone who genuinely wants to help people.

10 - Get a great accountant

Obviously ☺.